The
Radical Evangelical

Gospel & Culture (which incorporates The Gospel and Our Culture and the C. S. Lewis Centre) represents a coming together of Christians from many different churches and traditions, united by commitment to Jesus Christ and by a determination to engage with today's culture and to communicate the gospel to it.

We offer resources to help Christians to relate their faith to the real world. These include:

- Lecture tours, workshops and weekend conferences.
- Books, tapes, pamphlets and a journal, *Leading Light*.
- A meeting-point of Christians from a rich diversity of traditions, providing discussion, networking and support.

For more information, write to: Lavinia Harvey, **Gospel & Culture**, Dept of Theology and Religious Studies, King's College London, Strand, London WC2R 2LS.

The
Radical Evangelical
Seeking a Place to Stand

NIGEL WRIGHT

First published in Great Britain 1996
Society for Promoting Christian Knowledge
Holy Trinity Church
Marylebone Road
London NW1 4DU

British Library Cataloguing-in-Publication Data

A catalogue record of this book is available from
the British Library

ISBN 0-281-04952-1

Typeset by Pioneer Associates, Perthshire
Printed in Great Britain by
the Longdunn Press, Bristol

For
Hannah and Jonathan

Contents

1

In Defence of Labels

People do not like to be labelled. The reason is clear: labels can deny people's individuality. By lumping them together the ways in which they are distinct are overlooked. Suitably stereotyped, it becomes easier to neutralize and dismiss the challenge they represent. We all do it to others. We dislike it being done to ourselves.

Since labels have a bad name, on what grounds does a book like this advocate the label 'radical evangelical'? If labels are going to be used anyway, this is my preferred option. Life is complicated and is becoming more so. Theology and the spiritual life, contrary to rumours, are alive and well and increasing in diversity and complexity. Religion is not disappearing but mutating. It is too easy to be swept along or aside by the torrent. People need vantage-points to offer perspective in the midst of the flux. Amongst the various Christian positions, each of which may have its own integrity, there is one which I define as 'radical evangelical'. In this book I set out a reasoned, although personal, exposition of what it might involve, in order to clarify it for the already sympathetic and to commend it to others.

Theology is not just a question of finding a coherent system of thought: it is wisdom to live by. It is as important to have a theology which enables us to live well and to live generously as to have one free of internal contradictions. Wisdom is at a premium. There can be no doubt that some theologies prevent those who profess them from becoming wise, rounded and loving persons. In this book I set out a theological position which I believe to be both liberated and liberating.

Charting a course

To make this explicit, the book charts a course between the Scylla of liberalism and the Charybdis of fundamentalism. Yet clarification is needed here. Christianity contains certain fundamentals which are worth defending in a reasoned form. Those who think they can engage in major definitional change to the fundamentals and still claim continuity with the Christian faith need to think again. The word 'fundamentalism' has come, however, to refer to a mind-set, found not just in religion but in political, atheistic, artistic, feminist and other variations, which adheres to a particular world-view literalistically understood and not subject to criticism. Fundamentalisms produce people who are willing to impose their views on others through whatever means are open to them, ideological or governmental. This book resolutely opposes this mind-set and believes it to be contrary to Christ.

The book is equally opposed to liberalism and equally concerned to redeem the good word 'liberal'. In so far as being liberal denotes a generous attitude, a willingness to let others be, a hostility to oppression and an openness to others and their beliefs and convictions, including the insights of modernity, I have nothing to say against it and indeed would wish to argue for it. But again, 'liberalism' is something more than this. It is one thing to say that the biblical witness and the Church's confession need to be re-expressed in every age, and another to turn that witness and confession into something to be reshaped according to whichever moods and philosophies, modern or postmodern, dominate the scene. This is to deny that there is something strong, resilient and normative at the heart of the Church's convictions with the creativity to reconstruct our thought and life.

Fundamentalism and liberalism both obstruct the cause of Christ. Moreover, fundamentalism produces liberalism and vice versa. Large numbers of liberal Christians are refugee fundamentalists. Fundamentalism has the ability to convert and recruit, a capacity notably lacking in liberalism. Liberalism exists largely as a derivation from more robust forms of faith. By contrast, liberalism's reduction of Christian conviction calls for the strident counter-insistence of fundamentalism.

It has been claimed that conversion is the article by which the Christian faith stands or falls. Christianity is a missionary faith seeking to win others to freely given belief and commitment. To maintain its essential nature the Christian Church must be a community of conviction. Yet conviction is not the same as certainty. Certainty is an eschatological reality which comes from knowing Christ as we have been known. For the time being we see in part and know in part. The believer may have an inner assurance or witness of the Spirit that she or he is a child of God, but can never claim an absolute certainty, particularly not an intellectual one, for as long as we are called to live by faith and not sight. This preserves alongside the element of conviction that self-questioning modesty which prevents us claiming for our formulations of faith more than we are entitled to. We can be sure of Christ, but not so sure that our perceptions of him are any more than partial and limited. Yet, although we see in part, we *do* see.

Definitions and descriptions

To understand the term 'radical evangelical' we need to do some explaining. The evangelical tradition in the life of the Church is a diverse coalition of theologies, churches and ecclesial cultures. 'Evangelicalism' (certainly in the English-speaking world) can be described by its shared theological convictions, but is also heir to cultural forms and predispositions, specifically from Puritanism and Pietism. Puritanism developed in Britain in the sixteenth and seventeenth centuries as a movement of reform and renewal in the established churches. It was shaped by the teaching and practice of John Calvin and left indelible marks on the political and economic institutions of the European and Anglo-Saxon worlds. The Puritans took the Bible with immense seriousness and combined extensive theological enquiry with an emphasis on 'experimental' religion, lived and experienced faith. Pietism originated in Germany towards the end of the seventeenth century as a movement of renewal when Protestant Christianity was in danger of over-intellectualizing the faith. The Pietist stress was on the heart, on life rather than doctrine. Its influence was behind the Evangelical Revivals of the eighteenth century led by Whitefield and the Wesleys. Evangelical Christianity arose in the wake of these revivals and so combines particular doctrinal concerns with a strong emphasis on experience, particularly that of conversion.

A foremost historian of the evangelical movement, David Bebbington, finds, in what is becoming a classical definition,[1] that evangelicalism is distinguished by four qualities: *conversionism*, *activism, biblicism* and *crucicentrism*. *Conversion* occurs when the gospel is preached and sinners are awakened to their need and to the grace of God in Christ. It is accompanied by a recognition of sin and guilt. When conversion comes it brings joy, gratitude and release. It is not sufficient to undergo the processes of sacramental initiation. What counts is the personal encounter with God in Christ which brings transformation to human lives, the 'new birth' or the event of 'being saved'. From this experience derives the evangelical emphasis on witness and testimony.

The experience of conversion leads, not unnaturally, to *activism*. Those who have experienced conversion are apt to persuade and convince others to the same end. Hence the concern for evangelism, 'soul-winning', persuading others to give allegiance to Christ. The 'personal evangelist' is a highly valued type. The global evangelistic and missionary energy of evangelicals is truly astonishing. Evangelical culture is therefore generally activist rather than contemplative. It is verbal, entrepreneurial and enthusiastic. Evangelism is an unquestionable value for most evangelicals. Nor is it the case that this implies of necessity the neglect of social caring. Evangelicals have not lacked compassion or the desire to improve life for others and for most of their history have been both generous and innovative, even if sometimes they have lacked a sufficiently searching analysis of the causes of poverty.

Evangelical *biblicism* will occupy our attention at various points in this book. The Reformation watchwords of 'Christ alone, Scripture alone, faith alone and the glory of God alone' could well be taken as the banks within which the river of evangelicalism flows. It is a characteristic evangelical concern therefore to establish the doctrine and life of the Church on biblical foundations and to subject tradition to the criterion of biblical witness. In this sense evangelicalism is traditional Protestantism.

At this point, considerable varieties of emphasis emerge. There are those for whom church life must be formed only on the basis of what Scripture explicitly teaches and commands. Tradition is thus subjected to more far-reaching criticism and what cannot be explicitly legitimated from Scripture is rejected, often, of course, to be replaced by new traditions. Others are tolerant of whatever Scripture does not specifically forbid, so embracing elements of tradition that are not in conflict with any specific biblical teaching. More recent disagreements among evangelicals concern the

degree of literalness with which Scripture is to be interpreted and
the working out of an adequate understanding of both their
divine inspiration and their unambiguous humanity. A more
complex discussion surrounds the question of the interpretation
of Scripture and the observation that Christians with equal doctrinal commitment to its authority can nevertheless arrive at
diametrically opposed interpretations of its meaning and application. At a later point in this book we shall seek working solutions
to these issues.

Crucicentrism refers to the central focus that evangelicals give to
the atoning work of Christ upon the cross. This is, of course, part
of a complex of ideas including a heightened awareness of human
sinfulness and guilt and the reality of the wrath of God.
Evangelicals have stressed the work of Christ as both substitutionary and propitiatory, believing that Christ has borne the
judgement of God against human sin in such a way as to satisfy
both the divine justice and the divine compassion. In maintaining
these positions, evangelicals have often found themselves swim-
ming against the tide of 'progressive' theological opinion. This is
indeed an evangelical strength which this book will seek to illustrate and to emulate, the ability to resist temporary fashions for
the sake of continuity with the theological inheritance. Yet we
shall need to ask questions about the value of evangelical
approaches to the work of Christ and to explore their strengths
and weaknesses lest theology present a caricature of the redeeming work of God in Christ. We shall also be concerned to ask
whether in exalting the cross evangelicals have in fact restricted
its significance and made it a mechanism of salvation rather than
finding in it the key-signature both to the nature of the God
revealed at the cross and to the pattern of the Christian life.

Evangelical typology

Having explained, albeit in a preliminary way, what is meant by
the term 'evangelical', it becomes necessary to clarify the meaning of 'radical'. We may best do this by reviewing the types of
evangelicalism that are to be found and by locating the radical
evangelical in debate and disagreement with them.

Gabriel Fackre identifies two fundamental uses of the term
'evangelical'.[2] It refers in the first instance to the Protestant tradition generally. In this sense it denotes those who, at the time of

the Reformation, rediscovered the gospel as justification by grace through faith. Not surprisingly the Reformers were called evangelicals and, indeed, the cognate German term *evangelisch* is in use to this day to distinguish Protestants from Catholics. Subsequently the meaning of the term narrowed to refer to those who interiorized and intensified the experience of justification and of biblical authority. It refers to that stream of Protestantism in which personal conversion, a rigorous moral life, concentration on biblical authority and zeal for disseminating the faith are joined.

This fundamental distinction made, Fackre goes on to find six distinct sub-communities within the evangelical stream.[3] *Fundamentalist evangelicals* hold unswervingly to 'biblical inerrancy', the belief that the biblical text, being inspired by God, participates in the quality of divine life to the extent that it is without 'errors' of any type. The Bible is not only theologically true therefore, but *literally* true at every point on whatever subject it deals with, whether nature, history or doctrine. By mutual comparison, certain statements can be seen to be metaphorical in force, for instance, because 'God is spirit' anthropomorphic references to God are not taken literally. But the Bible can never be subjected to criticism from points outside itself, for instance modern science or understandings of history, since this would be to surrender its authority to earthly authorities, thereby denying its supremacy. Fundamentalism works with a high degree of literalism, not least in handling the apocalyptic passages of Scripture. It prizes as signs of correctness commitments to a 'creationist' rather than an evolutionist view of origins, Adam and Eve as the literal first human pair, a young earth, and the rejection of contemporary scholarly conclusions concerning the authorship or composition of biblical books. After years of isolation, fundamentalism has been making a comeback, especially in the USA, and is the backbone of what is sometimes called the religious or Christian Right.

Fackre's second and third categories are the *old evangelicals* and the *new evangelicals*. Old evangelicals put their stress upon the life of personal piety, individual morality and disciplined Bible study and have roots in significant theological traditions such as Dutch Calvinism. These themes are also found among new evangelicals, with additional concerns for the rational defence of the faith and a more aggressive approach to social issues. Both types are inclined towards biblical inerrancy but interpret it more broadly.

These categories would be recognized in the British context as 'conservative evangelicalism', a movement which has enjoyed a remarkable resurgence since World War II and grows from parties long present in the British Church. Conservative evangelicalism takes a conservative approach to the Scriptures but would by no means be tied to literalist interpretations or even necessarily to 'inerrancy'. It has, as Fackre indicates, become increasingly intellectually well resourced and socially and politically aware. One consequence of this is, almost inevitably, that its own boundaries are pushed out as those emerge from the movement who are committed to its core values yet are rethinking its traditional categories.

Fackre denotes as *justice and peace evangelicals* a minority, among whom Ron Sider and Jim Wallis are prominent, committed to a further-reaching critique of contemporary power structures than is traditionally the case among conservative evangelicals. This position notes that white evangelicals are often rooted in the prosperous and professional middle classes and so have a tendency to view the world with the concerns of that class. Unwittingly they can find themselves on the side of the oppressors. While possessing a strong sense of personal sin and morality, their individualism causes them to overlook the realities of structural or institutional sin; indeed they lack the kind of social analysis which would enable them to relate the gospel to that dimension.

Justice and peace evangelicals find that analysis in a reappropriation of the New Testament language concerning 'the powers'.[4] This term is held to include, although not to be exhausted by, social and political structures in human societies which are themselves estranged from their creator and their true purpose. They become oppressive and destructive. The Kingdom of God is correspondingly to be conceived as that divine action whereby the world is liberated in all its dimensions from its bondage to sin, fallenness and evil. The cross is not only the moment of atonement for human sin but also the action of God through Christ in overcoming the powers, breaking their hold over humans and restoring them under the risen Christ's rule, at least potentially, to their true and created intent as servants of human life not structures of domination over it.

This kind of analysis is certainly new territory for evangelicals, as indeed it is for Christian theology at large and human intellectual reflection generally. The disciplines of sociology and cultural analysis are relatively recent. The debt to Marxist analysis is also here discernible and Christian thinking shows that it is doing in the contemporary world what it has always done previously, namely sharpening its thinking by listening and responding to philosophy and culture. Now the voices are not those of Plato, Aristotle and the Enlightenment (all of which have had a huge impact on Christian theology, not least that of evangelicalism), but of today's social and psychological philosophers. It is here that one of the strengths of evangelical tradition manifests itself. Justice and peace evangelicals are able to draw upon earlier evangelical movements in which their concerns are anticipated. These include that sixteenth-century movement of radical Protestantism known as Anabaptism (partially represented today by the Mennonites and other 'historic peace churches') and variations within the Reformed strands of thought which have taken the civil realm and the so-called 'cultural mandate' with great seriousness. Once retrieved, there proves to be ample evidence in the tradition of both consistent action and profound thought concerning the relation of the gospel to social and political realms. Justice and peace evangelicals, although a minority voice (but increasingly and markedly less so), prove to be restoring what previously has been regarded as an essential part of the witness.

Fackre's fifth category touches on the most recent dimension of evangelicalism to emerge: *charismatic evangelicals*. Charismatic experience is by no means limited to evangelicals but it is particularly influential among them. The 'charismatic movement' represents the spreading into the historic denominations of experiences which were previously associated with Pentecostalism. Pentecostalism may itself be seen to be a development, at least in America, from within the Wesleyan, holiness tradition. John Wesley gave sanction to the experience of 'Christian perfection', the realization, even if only for a moment, of a state of entire sanctification before God. The tradition which flowed from this aspect of his teaching came to believe that, in addition and subsequent to conversion, crisis experiences of sanctification were possible. When Pentecostalism emerged after the Welsh and Asuza Street Revivals of 1904 and 1906, this crisis experience of 'baptism in the Holy Spirit' was understood as a moment of empowering and equipping rather than of sanctification, to be associated with speaking in tongues and other extraordinary phenomena such as healing, prophecy and 'words of knowledge'.

In the 1960s Pentecostal experiences began to spread more widely in the traditional denominations, giving rise to the charismatic movement which has in turn gone through a series of stages to the point where charismatic Christianity could on some predictions be poised to become the mainstream of evangelical faith and possibly even of Christianity itself in this country.[5] Contemporary evangelicalism cannot be understood without reference to this tendency.[6] There is no doubt, however, that this aspect of contemporary Christianity is its growing edge, and that many of the leaders, shapers and theological thinkers of the future will at least have passed *through* charismatic Christianity even if some have decided not to stay there.

Fackre's final category is that of *ecumenical evangelicals*, those who see evangelical faith within the broader stream of Christian belief and who avoid the forms of separatism or 'apartism' which evangelicals so easily adopt. Fackre's category here coincides closely with Richard Lovelace's description of 'unitive evangelicalism'.[7] We might identify here some who have emerged as significant contributors to both the missionary and the ecumenical movements, such as Max Warren and Bishops Stephen Neill, Lesslie Newbigin and Simon Barrington-Ward. Many such would be regarded with suspicion or even discounted by other evangelicals but in fact they are amongst the finest minds and noblest spirits of this tradition. Their intention is to hold together the various aspects of Christian mission in its evangelistic, social and political dimensions and to bond together the whole Church within the bounds of essential Christian orthodoxy.

Fackre's typology of evangelicals is helpful, but the categories he identifies are open, not closed. A recent book published by the Evangelical Alliance characterizes British evangelicalism as 'tribal', identifying twelve distinct tribes.[8] This is an appropriate judgement and intermarriage, trade and exchange between the tribes is considerable. For the purposes of the present book this makes it possible to see 'radical evangelicalism' as a tribal stream. But the question as to what 'radical' in this description might mean has not yet been answered.

The easiest thing to reaffirm, since we have already made the point, is that radical evangelicalism is not fundamentalism. Along with conservative evangelicalism,[9] we reject fundamentalism on account of its suspicion of scholarship, its literalist and wooden approaches to the Bible, its separatism and bondage to particular cultures, its apocalypticism and its identification with right-wing political agendas. Fundamentalism, while believing that it is remaining true to the Bible, actually has tied itself to the intellectual framework of a past era. If it is in tension with modern culture (and it is surprising how happily it can accommodate itself), it is so not because it is doggedly faithful to God as he has revealed himself to be in Christ and as the Scriptures bear enduring witness to him, but because it has sold itself out to cultures of a former day. It is an illusion to believe that this is conformity to Christ.

Conservative evangelicalism offers a better option. Its merit is its ability to rise above theological fashion, to maintain continuity with the sources of Christian authority in Scripture and tradition. Yet conservative evangelicalism has maintained a line in biblical study that has declared certain critical positions unacceptable. It has argued for the Mosaic authorship of the Pentateuch, the unity of Isaiah, an early date for the Book of Daniel, the entire historicity of the Fourth Gospel and the Pauline authorship of the Pastoral Epistles, as if the very Word of God is at stake over these issues.

New evangelicals have been more able to discriminate in the scholarly debates between what is of importance and what of relative indifference and have tended to advance mediating positions which accept the insights of modern critical study of the Bible without denying the essence of what conservative evangelicalism has stood for. So, to cite only one example, there is a greater willingness to accept what to me seems perfectly obvious, that the prophecy of Isaiah in its present form is not the product of one person but of several prophetic figures reinterpreting and reapplying the word of the Lord for greatly varying circumstances. Yet the book has a theological continuity and an integrity as a whole.

There is no doubt therefore that modern critical scholarship can enhance our reading of Scripture in ways unheard of for previous generations of the Church and we do well to acknowledge this and profit from it. Conservative evangelicalism has been in danger of attending to the *form* of Scripture while paying inadequate attention to its *content* as the Word of God. By assuming it knows what inspiration can and ought to imply for the form of Scripture it has been in danger of neglecting the primary duty of accepting the Bible as it actually is and attending to the Word of God which meets us there often in surprising ways.

Radical evangelicalism as I here seek to expound it is prepared to decide issues concerning the form of Scripture on their relative merits, not on the basis of a prior assumption about what the Bible must or may not be. It is not inherently suspicious of 'higher criticism'. This is a 'radical' position in that it is not wedded to the 'conservative' assumptions of much recent evangelicalism. It is radical in that it exhibits a greater willingness to let the Bible be *what it actually is*, rather than seeking to determine this in advance on the basis of *a priori* assumptions. In so far as 'conservative' evangelicalism is no longer that conservative but has allowed itself the freedom to push out the boundaries and has begun to think with new degrees of creative imagination, radical evangelicalism is a development from this 'tribe'.

As this book proceeds, my own indebtedness to some of the radical aspects of evangelical history will emerge, in particular that type of radical Protestantism which has taken form first in Anabaptism and then in the Free Churches of English history. Yet the position I develop, while drawing on the resources of the past, should not be seen as the restatement of a past position but as a position appropriate for the present moment, addressing certain questions which our forebears may not have confronted in the same way. It is with justice and peace evangelicals and with ecumenical evangelicals that radical evangelicals are probably most at home. The emphasis on response to the content of the Word of God, rather than secondary debates about its form, and upon radical social action in continuity with the action of Jesus the Messiah, are here deemed to have priority. Justice and peace evangelicals stress that Christ's journey to the cross is the revelation of the way in which above all other ways God overcomes evil. By confronting evil and yet refusing to respond to it *in its own terms* even though this means the suffering of the cross, God overcomes it. In continuity with this, Christians are called to make justice not by seizing power over society in order that by means of such power they might eradicate evil, but by confronting evil in the name and Spirit of Christ. Power does tend to corrupt, but, as Jesus abundantly illustrates, there can be an enormous moral power in powerlessness which has long-term transformative potential even though in the short term it may be defeated. This insight, which most Christians would accept as the distinctively Christian way of behaving on the personal level, can actually be translated (although admittedly not simplistically) into a form of political action. It can be the way of making social justice and advancing earthly peace. Christians are to imitate Jesus in identifying with the downtrodden, oppressed and poor. The God of the Bible is biased to the poor and so should be his Church.[10] This constitutes the Church in the world not as a bastion of the *status quo* or legitimator of the present order, but as a radical, transforming presence with a clear sense that the 'powers' need to be subverted in order that they might be restored to their true order in the economy of God.

In prospect

The Evangelical Alliance in Great Britain has the one hundred and fiftieth anniversary of its founding in 1996. Evangelical achievements will be celebrated, no doubt with a due sense of equal or greater evangelical failures. Inevitably and appropriately there will be talk of evangelical diversity and of the freedom, without which no coalition can endure, of private judgement. The position outlined in this book is self-consciously and gladly on the left of the evangelical spectrum. In the course of these chapters we shall touch upon issues such as the status of the Bible, the nature of Christ's achievement on the cross, the meaning of 'hell' and the 'larger hope' for the salvation of humankind, all of which have been areas of persistent evangelical disagreement and controversy for well over a hundred years.

I do not imagine that the book will escape criticism. Yet it is so fashioned as to argue not only that it represents a legitimate hue in the evangelical rainbow but that the reflections it contains might be enriching for all evangelical believers and others. The gospel we profess is the most radical power on earth, reaching to the depths of our personal, social and political existence. It needs a radical people to embody and proclaim it.

2

Revolutionary Orthodoxy

Evangelicals are party people. They easily divide the world into those who are 'for' or 'against' what they stand for. In former generations this was indicated by the over-use of the word 'sound'. A 'sound' person was one who scored high in the approval ratings on subjects like biblical inerrancy, supernaturalism, belief in hell and penal substitution. Disagreement in these areas could constitute a 'sound barrier'! Evangelicals were early practitioners of political correctness in expecting their adherents and especially spokespeople to be ideologically pure. Deviation could lead to someone's evangelical credentials being questioned. Recent years have seen a pushing out of the boundaries, but echoes of the 'kosher/non-kosher' mind-set can still be traced.

The truth here is that Christianity cannot be subject to limitless redefinition without ceasing to be itself. Its shortcoming is the disposition to set limits prematurely, to regard differences of interpretation as departures from orthodoxy. In this chapter I argue that the fundamental, defining paradigm by which we interpret Christianity is the trinitarian doctrine of God. Where God is sincerely confessed as Father, Son and Spirit we find the apostolic faith and fellow believers. Conversely, when this understanding of God is rejected, the Christian faith has been deserted. Yet paradoxically, this 'conservatism' leads to the most radical conclusions.

The primacy of the Trinity

The trinitarian doctrine of God is the historic core of Christian worship, experience and theology. The earliest creeds, including the Apostles' Creed, are divided into three clauses relating to God the Father Almighty, Jesus Christ his only Son our Lord and the Holy Spirit. This confession reaches back into the deep structure of Christian revelation. It reflects the shape of God's redeeming actions in history, first for Israel, then in Christ and then through the Holy Spirit.

The Christian faith grew in the first instance out of an encounter with God, an assurance of being drawn by the Spirit through the Son to the Father. In this encounter it became necessary, and inevitable, that the meaning of the word 'God' should undergo creative redefinition. God's unity was not singularity but a unity of perfect communion and mutual indwelling of divine persons. To be sure, it is still necessary to give primacy to the Father as the fountain and source of deity, the one from whom the Son and Spirit derive their being eternally and who expresses his infinite fullness through them. But at root God is not isolated singularity but communion and mutual self-giving. At the heart of all things there is a loving, personal, relational reality from whom life and love overflow for all.

This vision of God is so revolutionary that we have to stretch our words and concepts to capture its energy. Preconceived notions of 'God' from whatever source are here subjected to radical reworking, especially so when the additional claim is made that God is most clearly revealed to us not in nature but in the cross of Christ. At this horrific place, who and what we consider God to be is reconstructed from the bottom up. God is *most of all* to be found in the cross of Christ. Here we glimpse the painful love with which he loves his free creatures, his willingness to enter into and bear their alienation and their sin in order to reconcile them to himself. This God associates with the lowly, the rejected, the outcast and the godforsaken, and reverses our assumptions about how gods, or fathers, or kings and rulers ought to be. He defines himself as the humble God who, whatever his undoubted powers to rule over and dispose of his creation, is most truly himself as he has shown himself to be in Christ and his cross.

This revolutionary vision is jeopardized and lost once the doctrine of the Trinity is discarded. Christ exists as the image of the Father,[1] who makes the Father known within the conditions of humanity,[2] who knows God and so can mediate that knowledge to others.[3] The full realization of the doctrine of Christ's deity is anticipated in the New Testament's witness to the uncomplicated worship of Christ by his people.[4] Christ is to be worshipped as God manifest in the flesh. The converse of the deity of Christ is thus the Christlikeness of the deity. The trinitarian vision finds hope for humanity in the fact that God himself has participated through Christ in the human condition, thereby renewing humankind from within and so empowering others to realize the divine intention for their lives in communion with himself. God has invested himself in human salvation. He has shown himself to be the passionate God whose love for his creation means that his passion is warm and tender.[5] In all the distress of his people he too is distressed.[6] Furthermore, the Spirit who comes through Christ is the personal presence of God which breathes through all creation and through whom God dwells in and with his people so that they can be called the 'dwelling place' of God.[7] The transcendent God has taken creaturehood to himself by becoming part of his creation in the person of his Son, and he also dwells as Spirit in the depths as the power which undergirds all things, realizing his purpose from within and drawing creation to its goal.

A paradigm shift too far

This is a radical vision of God which is not to be surrendered and especially not in the name of the kind of 'radical theology' which is advanced from time to time and which turns out not to be radical at all.

There is a persistent current in Western theology which has argued that to become 'relevant' theology needs to undergo a 'paradigm shift'. Christian theology, as any other human intellectual discipline, has certainly undergone periodic paradigm shifts.[8] The fundamental framework within which theology is conceived changes as a consequence of accumulating forces or processes acting upon it. In scientific theory, by comparison, the Copernican revolution signalled a fundamental transition from conceiving the earth as the centre of the universe to seeing it as a minor star in a solar system whose centre is elsewhere. Newton and Einstein likewise have mediated subsequent shifts of perception. In each paradigm shift fundamental elements of previous paradigms are carried over into the new, yet the framework or angle of perception through which they are viewed changes so that the individual elements are perceived in a somewhat different way.

Theology cannot be developed independently from shifts of thought in other areas of human enquiry and must relate itself to those changes. It is sometimes suggested, with justification, that theology has progressed from a mythological or narrative phase, in which stories were paramount as vehicles of truth, to an onto-logical or metaphysical phase, under the influence of Greek philosophy and its concern for abstract formulations of truth, to a rational and empirical phase under the concerns of the Enlightenment and the scientific revolution, and so to a relational phase, under the influence of the behavioural sciences. Attention turns to where the next paradigm shift may take us.

One persistent challenge concerns a shift whereby the historic Christian claim to be making true statements about the objective reality and actions of a personal God is surrendered in favour of a recognition that all religious language is metaphorical in nature. Christianity should not claim to be propounding objective truth but to be a tradition of impressionistic responses to an essentially mysterious divine reality, a tradition in which the symbols and images employed are held to express aspects of human experience, but no more than this. Prominent within this latter tendency is the Anglican priest Don Cupitt and the 'Sea of Faith' movement within Anglicanism.

A tradition of Christian reconstruction goes back to the eigh-teenth-century Enlightenment and was classically expressed by Friedrich Schleiermacher.[9] Schleiermacher attempted to salvage a place for religion in an age when it was on the run. The Enlightenment paradigm shift towards the exaltation of reason, the rejection of traditional authorities, and the principle of doubt, meant that religion had to justify itself before the bar of certain newly prominent epistemological criteria. As religion does not conform to scientific means of analysis and its truth cannot be substantiated through empirical means, Schleiermacher's project entailed finding a basis for religion in the 'experience of absolute dependence'. Christian doctrines were reconstructed as ways of expressing this religious experience. Contemporary advocates of a merely metaphorical view of religious truth follow the same pattern of thought. It is not doubted that human beings have religious experiences: this is a universal and well-substantiated phenomenon. The problem concerns how such experiences are understood and the status of the claims to which they give rise. To illustrate this theme we draw attention to three contemporary advocates of this general position, although it should be noted that each of them develops their position for dissimilar reasons and with differing nuances.

a. *Abandoning 'finality'*

John Hick, for instance, no longer finds it possible in the light of our knowledge of other faiths to believe in the traditional claims of Christianity.[10] Hick is entirely right to see that such claims, embodied in the Scriptures, in the Church's liturgy and hymns, and systematized in its doctrines and creeds, imply that through Christ there is a unique access to God and his saving activity. It is hard to avoid the inference, the claim runs on, that Christianity is 'superior' to other faith traditions. This can in turn be used as an instrument for asserting the superiority of certain nations, peoples or races above others. The doctrine of the Trinity, with which we are concerned above all other things in this chapter, is a case in point. If it is objectively true, Christians possess a knowledge of God not shared by others, including Jewish believers. Such exclusive claims are unacceptable in today's world since increasingly it becomes clear that the experience of the divine is not the exclusive possession of Christians and that others from non-Christian traditions love God and express that love through devoted lives.

Hick's alternative to traditional Christian belief does not include the wholesale rejection of the Christian tradition but the recognition that it is a tradition of response to that divine reality which is common to the religious experience of all humanity. The exclusive claims within which Christianity is packaged, and which may have been excusable in previous generations, must now be seen to be questionable, and are best quietly left behind in the onward evolution of the religion. As interpretation of the Bible has undergone a paradigm shift under the influence of the scientific revolution, so that we make mental adjustments when we read of God being 'in heaven' and no longer believe this to be a literal location but a metaphorical way of speaking, so we should see that our doctrinal language is merely 'a way of speaking' and is not literally true. Christianity needs to leave behind the theology of exclusiveness in favour of a universal vision of the divine.[11]

There is an initial attractiveness to this position which is partly due to Hick's clarity of exposition and his very evident compassion. His project reflects his own movement out of evangelical

Christianity into something broader. He has personally undergone a paradigm shift, in large measure because of his concern
to assert the love of God for his whole human creation and his
universal will-to-save. Critics may wish to question aspects of his
account.[12] It does contain a fundamental irony in that even while
rejecting Christian claims to unique knowledge, it is making
exactly the same claim for itself. For Hick, and those like him, is
actually claiming to have a superior knowledge about that reality
with which religions are concerned and about the language by
means of which it is described. He understands that religions are
not, as their exponents mistakenly believe, objectively true, but
only metaphorically so. A position which promises to be something new, in actuality proves to be the same as what is criticized:
a claim to privileged access to knowledge, insight and understanding. Hick's programme then becomes one more amongst
the many competing claims to truth, and instead of bringing
resolution to the matter of religious diversity simply adds to it. It
contains all the same potential to be a vehicle of intolerance as do
more traditional systems. While promising to avoid intellectual
imperialism, this is precisely what it seeks; and it is the more
deceptive in that it pursues this goal covertly.

The paradigm shift that Hick advocates makes religion acceptable within that intellectual framework called 'modernity' (that
mood and pattern of thought which has developed out of the
Enlightenment shift in the ways Westerners think): reason is the
supreme arbiter of truth; claims to normative or determinative
access to divine revelation are rejected; no religious truth claims
are ultimately true because they cannot be tested by scientific
criteria; religious convictions may be held firmly, provided that
they are kept in the private or tribal realm and make no bid for
public acceptance; they are expressions of the religious consciousness, not descriptions of the way things actually are; tolerance
and pluralism are ultimate values. Hick is recasting traditional
belief to make it acceptable to this new framework. I shall in due
course argue that this attachment to current cultural modes of
thought is inherently conservative, not radical, and loses the
revolutionary character of trinitarian thought.

b. *Abandoning 'patriarchy'*

A further example of the shift from orthodox, trinitarian
Christianity is represented by the feminist theologian, Daphne

Hampson.[13] She differs from Hick in that whereas he still considers himself a Christian Hampson describes herself very firmly as a 'post-Christian', although still very much a religious believer, one of a growing number who have come to the conclusion that Christianity is neither true nor moral.[14] It cannot be true because Hampson accepts as axiomatic the Enlightenment assumption and observation that the causal nexus between events cannot be interrupted. This rules out the possibility of miracle and specifically of the resurrection. And if Christ is not raised then even by its own account Christianity is not true. However, this exposure of Christianity as untrue acts for Hampson as a liberation since it sets her free no longer to feel tied, as once she did, to certain past moments of history, such as the history of Israel's religion, to Christ and the New Testament. Instead she becomes free to construct her religion in the present in the same way that she, or anybody, engages in any other intellectual pursuit: she can draw from the past that which is helpful without feeling bound to adhere to that in the tradition which is uncongenial for life in the present. This is significant for her in overcoming the male-dominated legacy of Christianity and entering into her identity as a woman.

This approach is intimately tied in with another axiomatic element in Hampson's religion, which again comes from the Enlightenment, commitment to the fundamental equality of human beings, male or female. Hampson finds in the Christian Scriptures, in Christ and in the Christian tradition a lamentable and irredeemable patriarchalism. The consequence is that wherever the Christian Scriptures are read or Christianity spreads, a subtle (and sometimes blatant) devaluing of women takes place such that Christianity has to be rejected as immoral, that is, regressive in its influence on the quest of women and men for emancipation and true equality. The fact that Christianity can be exposed now as untrue frees us to reject the oppressive shackles that it imposes. Whatever value Christianity had in the past, and she acknowledges that it certainly has acted as a vehicle for expressing love for God, that value has now been outlived. And Hampson is as critical of Christian feminists as she is of Christianity itself. A male religion which takes as its point of reference certain historical moments in patriarchal societies is beyond repair as a vehicle of women's spirituality in the present. Christian feminists, who are tinkering with the mere fringes of Christianity in search of a modicum of comfort in it, are refusing to address the inescapable questions concerning its fundamental truth.

Like Hick, Hampson invites us to a paradigm shift which moves beyond historic Christianity. Also like him she wishes to retain a profound belief in God and, as emerges in her work, love for God and spiritual depth. Unlike him she recognizes that Christianity must be acknowledged to be either true or false. Redefining the sense in which it is true (so Hick) or recasting the language through which it is mediated (so Christian feminism's attempts to feminize the deity), just will not work. Love of God has in times past and present found expression even through the flawed vehicle of Christianity but religious experience is greater than Christianity and is a profound reality. Yet Hampson's own turn from the tradition of her upbringing has also freed her from the necessity to view the divine as personal or even as something to which she should bow down and worship, since this is demeaning of human value. Instead, the divine (which itself defies definition) is perceived in, through and beyond the realities of the created world.[15]

Hampson certainly offers a trenchant attack (for such it is) upon Christianity. The work is the more compelling in that she has been an insider, an active Christian employing the arguments of the Christian faith, yet she has now lost faith in them. An admirably honest thinker and writer, she concedes that her case collapses if it is indeed the case that Christ has risen. And yet such a possibility is ruled out *a priori* and without further comment via the axiom that the causal nexus between events cannot be interrupted. At this point, and in her equally axiomatic commitment to equality (interpreted, it seems, in the specific way she determines), her own absolute commitments are laid bare. These commitments then determine the rest of her argument. Once more we note the unquestioning commitment to certain Enlightenment axioms, to which we shall return.

c. *Abandoning 'objectivity'*

A third example of the call for a further paradigm shift can be found in the book by the Anglican priest Anthony Freeman which received considerable attention in the media.[16] Freeman differs from both Hick and Hampson in that in rejecting the traditional categories of the Christian faith he also flatly denies the ontological existence of any reality that we might call God other than that 'God' we create for ourselves by the values according to which we

seek to live. The underlying assumption of his work is that 'observations made within the natural world can give us no information
about anything beyond the natural world'.[17] This axiom provides
no basis on which, either through natural or special revelation, it
makes sense to speak of God. It resembles Gotthold Lessing's
eighteenth-century 'ugly broad ditch', according to which it is
impossible to argue from the accidental facts of history to a
necessary truth of reason. All Christian claims to truth thus fall
at the first hurdle, being ruled out as claims to truth from first
principles.

The novelty in Freeman's book is that despite Christianity's not
being true in any objective sense, it continues to represent for him
a system of values kept alive through the liturgical and doctrinal
traditions of Christianity. Freeman's desire is thus to continue as
a priest, practising all the aspects of traditional Christian religion
while conceiving of it all in a purely humanistic or naturalistic
sense as a way of setting human lives in the context of particular,
'Christian' values. He can even advance the audacious claim that
by holding this position he is the true inheritor of authentic
Christianity, especially of the Church of England, and that the
'zealots' who actually continue to believe it are usurpers! While
differing from Hampson and Hick concerning the actual reality
of 'God', he nonetheless values religious experience and indicates
that even within the dimension of the merely human there are
mysteries we do not yet comprehend.

Each of these writers advocates a paradigm shift within or beyond
traditional Christianity. The shift enables them to carry over into
the new paradigm whatever is deemed to be of value in the old
without being bound by its limiting aspects. What is considered
unacceptable in the old is determined for each of them by their
encounter with the values and axioms of modernity. This is clearest in Freeman for whom modernity acts as a criterion of truth.
Frequently he rejects the traditional content of the faith on the
grounds that 'we cannot believe that any more' or 'this makes no
sense to us today'. In more sophisticated and theologically profound terms the same adherence to the assertions of modernity is
visible in Hick and Hampson. I wish to argue that this methodology while claiming to be radical is in fact both conformist and
conservative and that the true radicalism is shown by those who
hold fast to authentic Christianity. It is conservative because each

of these thinkers, and those who adopt their methods, are making contemporary culture the actual shaping authority for their work. While rejecting orthodox Christianity for its particularity they are taking the particular, not to say parochial, axioms of a small segment of human intellectual history as absolutes.

Theology and the 'adversary culture'

A justified criticism of historic Christianity is that it has often so accommodated itself to the wealthy and powerful in human societies as to become a legitimating ideology for the powerful. It has in the manner of most religions become a conservative force within society. This happens when Christianity confines itself to the personal and individual and avoids challenging the social conditions of humankind. It is also the case that the radical elements of the gospel, which inevitably assert themselves wherever the Scriptures are read and the subversive memory of Jesus recalled, have given rise to protest movements against the establishment. There is an honourable history of non-conformist movements of many kinds. When the bondage of Christianity to culture is referred to, it is usually with a view to exposing the role of Christianity as a conservative force. I wish to point to another tendency however.

Since World War II there has been in the Western world an unprecedented explosion of prosperity with considerable social implications. Sociologists have come to distinguish two cultures within the expanding middle classes: one is concerned with the production of goods and corresponds to the old manufacturing bourgeoisie, the other with the production of symbolic knowledge and representing those engaged, for instance, in university teaching, social work, the media, cultural and aesthetic activities.[18] This new 'knowledge class' élite tends to come into conflict with the 'business class' and develops an anti-bourgeois, adversary culture from within which arise the so-called 'new social movements' which are typically concerned with the autonomous self, 'tolerance' and liberation. From within the adversary culture arises the impetus for feminism, abortion rights reform, environmental concern, anti-discrimination legislation, gay rights and similar concerns. It is from within this culture that the call for a paradigm shift in theology also tends to arise and its advocates can be seen to be the product of it. When Freeman therefore refers to what

modern people find it possible or impossible to believe, he does not have in mind the totality of the human population, the majority of which seems to have little difficulty believing all manner of 'unmodern' things; nor does he mean the general run of Western populations who, on enquiry, appear also to have a more flexible and open world-view. He is referring to that particular segment of the middle classes to which he belongs, whose values and axioms appear to him to be self-evidently true and which he somewhat imperialistically deems to be an adequate and indubitable grid through which to view the world.

Now it is not part of my intention to take issue with the individual issues that arise within the new social movements or to reject their agendas, with many of which I would be sympathetic. I do wish to point out that even while claiming to be radical, the theological positions we have examined in fact exhibit a form of conformism in that they are the expression and the theological legitimation of the concerns and ethos of the 'knowledge class' and new social movements. We therefore have a phenomenon that directly parallels the alliance of Christianity with the bourgeoisie, but this time it is an alliance with the adversary culture. The concerns of the new social movements are taken to be self-evidently true and constitute an authority which overrules that of tradition or even of the Christian Scriptures. Yet at the heart of this acceptance of the authority of culture there are commitments of faith, the acceptance of certain unproven axioms (for Hampson the causal nexus between events cannot be broken; for Freeman observations made within the natural world can yield no information about anything beyond) which themselves depend upon nothing but upon which everything else depends. It is no surprise that once accepted these axioms lead away from traditional Christianity, but it should be noted that they are accepted *a priori* and without argument and then used as the criteria by which other matters should be judged.

The irony is that as these theologians advocate the acceptance of the axioms of modernity as a shaping authority, many others are questioning them. 'Postmodernism', whatever else it is or is not, is at least that mood whereby the limited and questionable nature of modernity is acknowledged in the light of its own criteria. It was after all only a matter of time before the criterion of doubt would apply itself to the criterion of doubt. Where the Enlightenment philosopher Gotthold Lessing once proclaimed that the accidental facts of history cannot yield the necessary truths of reason, postmodernism is up-ending his judgement and proclaiming that the so-called 'necessary truths of reason' are *nothing but* accidental facts of history. Dominant opinion turns out on examination to be simply one more subculture and not a privileged source of truth for everyone.[19]

By surrendering the independence of the theological enterprise and subjecting its authority to the authority of culture, those who advocate a paradigm shift ensure that they will be able to offer nothing back to culture save what it already knows and believes, this time decked out in religious garb. This is hardly radical. Nor is it exciting. By holding fast to its own sources of authority in Christ, Scripture, tradition and spiritual experience, theology is able by contrast to subject to an independent criticism the values of both the business class and of the knowledge class (and indeed of any other 'class') and be bound to neither. To be sure, this Christ came to us clothed in the culture of a first-century Jew, but at the same time transcending both that culture and all cultures since. This is a *conservative* position in that it holds fast to Christ as traditionally confessed. But it is *radical* in that it cuts to the roots of all opinions and subjects them to judgement in the light of Christ. Those who dispense with *this* Christ in favour of a pale imitation doom themselves to conformity.

The radical Trinity

Admittedly the position for which I have argued is a faith position: at its heart it is a decision to accept Christ as the shaping authority, and not another. Yet a similar commitment of faith to accept certain axioms or ultimately unprovable realities which then determine the outcome is, as we have seen, at the heart of any position. In this sense the risk of believing in Christ as the very Word of God is that foolishness which in time by the sense it makes of life, the universe and everything proves to be the very wisdom of God.[20] There would be nothing 'foolish' about this at all if it did not in considerable measure run counter to what generally passes for wisdom. I do not on this score underestimate the challenge that Hick and Hampson in particular represent. Their positions and arguments are worthy of great respect. Furthermore, there are pressures and stresses which accrue for any 'cognitive minority', which is what orthodox Christians now are in our culture, which has a different starting-point for understanding the world from the majority cultures in which it is set and so holds a world-view at variance with them. I wish now to argue that trinitarian Christianity is not only a more radical stance towards culture but also that it is ultimately more liberating, and liberation is a primary value of the new social movements.

My argument has so far been that the paradigm shift which goes beyond orthodox Christian doctrine is inevitably a barren and a non-radical one. To fulfil its radical and revolutionary vocation the Christian faith requires a paradigm shift which develops more fully the implications of its trinitarian doctrine of God. Parallel to the call for a paradigm shift in theology away from orthodoxy, there has been an astonishing renewal of interest in the doctrine of the Trinity, the very essence of orthodoxy, the results of which have been brilliantly summarized by a study commission of the former British Council of Churches in the report *The Forgotten Trinity*.[21] This helps us to find the way forward.

Drawing upon the seminal work of John Zizioulas,[22] the report roots the doctrine of the Trinity in the primary experience of Christian worship of the Father by the Spirit through the Son. The being of God consists in God's communion as Father, Son and Spirit. It is a fully personal communion in which the persons of the Trinity are constituted by means of the relations between them. This insight concerning the being of God provides the grammar, or the key-signature, for exploring the whole of reality.[23] The world is the product not of chance, nor of an overbearing and coercive deity conceived of in essentially impersonal terms (and which Western philosophy has found it necessary to reject because of its stifling nature), but of a free and personal God who invites and enables his creatures to fulfil the potential of their own personhood through sharing in relationship with himself and with others. This conflicts with the essential individualism and autonomy of the Enlightenment inheritance and substantiates the view that truly personal existence is only possible because of communal relations.[24] In turn this provides the key for understanding the Church as *koinonia*, the 'ikon' of the Trinity bodying forth the 'perichoretic' relations of the Trinity, that is to say, that reality by which the divine persons indwell and interpenetrate one another in a communion of love.[25] The Church exists as communion before ever it takes form as institution and has the nature of mutuality rather than hierarchy, but a mutuality in which what we supply to each other through our relations and patterns of interdependence is paramount.

It becomes possible to see how the doctrine of the Trinity offers insights into the nature of human social existence. Whereas a purely monotheistic doctrine might be used to legitimate monarchy or dictatorship, for human social existence to be fashioned in the image of God it must reflect the pattern of persons-in-relation. All social and political systems which treat people as less than persons or whose essence is coercion come under judgement. The Church's existence as a communion based on love thus becomes a political challenge to unjust or impersonal systems.[26] Persons have priority. In this, some of the legitimate and necessary concerns of modernity, the commitment to human rights for instance, are substantiated theologically. Yet at the same time the lack of attention to human duties and obligations which human rights language can reflect is corrected by a corresponding stress upon what we owe to each other in the human family.

Moreover, the feminist criticism, such as Hampson represents, which rejects Christian teaching because of the supposed 'maleness' of the deity, neglects the way in which at a deeper theological level the doctrine of the Trinity is also about the task of reinterpreting what it means to be male. The nurturing, humble, self-giving Father who is of the same nature as Christ and is revealed in him, is far from being the legitimator of patriarchal systems but is their judge. The God who is 'all in all' is not exhausted by the language of fatherhood, or of motherhood for that matter, but is the quintessential fulfilment of both *and much more besides*. As the 'wholly other', not a creation of humans in their own image, he both brings into judgement and redefines sinful and finite categories of thought and language. A truly liberating feminism is therefore to be found not by rejecting the doctrine of the triune God but by entering more profoundly into its inner logic.

Certainly, as a response to Hick, to deny the doctrine of the Trinity for the sake of a hoped-for harmony with non-Christian faith traditions would represent a loss of essential integrity. But the doctrine itself, through its emphasis on personhood achieved through relations, indicates the more difficult and yet ultimately more enriching path to follow: dialogue with those of other faiths must be a truly relational and personal activity in which, on the basis of a common humanity and a shared quest, otherness and differences are made visible and accepted. So comes mutual enrichment as human beings live for and with each other and journey on the road towards a new humanity.[27]

When the trinitarian doctrine of God was first formulated in the early ecumenical councils of the Christian Church, the enormous task which faced this young but cogent community was how to take the language and categories of thought which belonged to surrounding culture and adapt them as vehicles of Christian truth. This task was stunningly accomplished by adhering tenaciously to the belief that the eternal God had become incarnate for human salvation in Jesus Christ. The particularity of Christianity, the value it invests in certain disreputable historical events and in one supreme historical person, has always been its offensiveness to its cultured despisers, 'a stumbling block to Jews and foolishness to Greeks'.[28] One way of solving the problem of religious pluralism is indeed to water down the specificity of Christ.[29] But to those who take the more radical risk, Christ becomes both wisdom and power.

Conclusion

The primary debate in the Church of today is not between evangelicals and non-evangelicals but between those who hold fast to the trinitarian core of Christian faith and those who wish to depart from it. Christianity itself and the possibility of being truly radical are at stake in this debate. Evangelicals will certainly range themselves on the side of revolutionary orthodoxy. They need eyes to see that 'those on our side are more than those on theirs'[30] and work in affirming coalition with all those who confess the apostolic faith. These are the boundaries that most matter and evangelicals should be careful not so to draw them that they weaken the very cause in which they firmly believe.

3

God's Universal Outreach

The doctrine of the Trinity provides the foundation for all other Christian doctrines. Traditionally evangelicals have made particular doctrines such as biblical infallibility, penal substitution, and eternal judgement the boundaries between 'sound' and 'unsound' theology. I have argued that the proper 'centre stage' is the trinitarian doctrine of God, and all other aspects radiate from this centre.

Evangelicals perceive an enemy of good theology in 'universalism', belief in the final redemption of all creatures. It therefore becomes difficult to avoid a negative dimension in either theology or Christian practice. Perhaps this is inevitable for any faith which believes in divine judgement. The question is whether it becomes excessive and what kind of people it might then form. The negative always has a tendency to displace the positive. This is particularly so at the popular level at which the nuances and caveats of more sophisticated theological discussion can be lost. In this chapter I shall argue that the negative dimension in popular and traditional evangelicalism is excessive, but not because we are entitled to be more optimistic about human beings than evangelicals allow; rather because the negative elements are not securely placed within a trinitarian narrative of creation, redemption and consummation which is conceived as the highest and final reality.

Discerning the negative dimension

Evangelicals incline towards a pessimistic judgement of human nature. Often this is expressed by saying that people are 'basically

28

evil'. Human nature is, in traditional Calvinist language, 'totally depraved'. Not surprisingly this disposes many to a strong conviction of the need for law and order. Paradoxically, and also following Calvin at this point, a low view of individual human morality is accompanied by a relatively high view of the ability of the forces of law and order not to act in a depraved manner. The strong belief in human sinfulness is of course balanced by an equally strong conviction that all human beings are made in the image of God and so are of infinite value. However, as the negative tends to displace the positive, it is a pessimistic view of humankind which frequently comes to the fore.

Evangelicals believe that human beings, being born in sin, are on their way to hell from the very beginning. Apart from divine grace and intervention, all who are without Christ are lost in this life and will be lost in eternity unless they repent and believe. This dire scenario is presented as the motivation for mission, with the emphasis on what lies beyond this life rather than how we live within it. Even the total number of nominal adherents to Christian churches is a minority of the whole human population. Moreover, evangelicals are resolute that only those who are truly born of the Spirit are among the redeemed, and this is a minority within the minority who have formally been received into the churches through sacramental action. There is therefore only a relatively small proportion of the sinful mass of humanity whose eternal destiny is secure. When to this is added the belief that eternal destinies are determined in this life, since 'it is appointed to mortals to die once, and after that the judgment'[1] and in eternity a huge chasm is fixed between the blessed and the damned which 'no one can cross',[2] it becomes difficult to avoid the conclusion that the majority of the human race is destined for and ends up in hell. It is relevant here to underline that the traditional evangelical belief, consistent with the consensus of the Church up until the modern era, is that hell consists of eternal, conscious torment. Unless this basic theological position is attenuated we are confronting the scenario of most human beings who have ever lived suffering an eternal conscious damnation in hell-fire. I think this could be described as pessimistic.

Unfortunately we have not yet finished plumbing the depths of the negative dimension. It would be a common judgement among evangelicals that all non-Christian religions are at best misguided and at worst demonic and that the world at large is under the domination of Satan, the archetypal power of evil. In this sense the only 'safe' realm is within the Church, although even here there are those who find sufficient room for demons to afflict and possess people. Evangelicals have been particularly impressed and shaped by the apocalyptic strands of biblical literature which employ bizarre and highly drawn images to make their point. Taken literally, apocalyptic yields a picture of the destruction of the earth, the heavens being set ablaze and the elements being melted by fire.[3] Salvation is therefore conceived of as individuals being rescued from the wrath to come,[4] as brands plucked from the burning,[5] delivered from the final destruction which is to come upon the earth. It is hard to avoid in this an incipient dualism and 'survivalist' mentality: salvation means being rescued from an earth which is on its way to destruction. The hope for improvement in earthly existence is finally a forlorn one.

It might be objected that the picture I have painted describes *fundamentalism* at its most lurid but is not entirely fair to *evangelicalism*. This is a fair comment. Even if most evangelicals do not hold to the picture in the exact form in which I have described it, however, many do hold fast to elements of it, and even those who distinguish themselves from it have it as the inherited backdrop against which their own theology is worked out. Mark Noll has pointed out that the 'mental habits' of fundamentalism continue in evangelicalism:

> The fundamentalist era remains critical for evangelical thinking, since it so thoroughly established habits of mind for looking (or not looking) at the world. It greatly encouraged a set of intellectual instincts that still, after a century filled with change, exert a pervasive influence over the thinking of evangelicals.[6]

My suggestion is that the picture I have painted exercises a gravitational pull on much evangelical thought. Many evangelicals resist it by chipping away at elements within the edifice. So, for instance, the doctrine of eternal conscious torment is questioned, or the possibility of gaining salvation through 'general revelation' is considered. Significant though each of these discussions is, the basic issue concerns the point from which we start. The starting-point determines the outcome, and what is required is a task of fundamental theological reconstruction in certain areas.

Calvinism and Arminianism

There can be no doubt that the Bible portrays salvation as the gracious gift of God and ascribes the initiative in human redemption entirely to him. This is a fundamental biblical theme and has given rise to a 'great debate' in theology, not only in Protestantism, concerning the divine initiative and its implications.[7] Given that not all human beings come within their lifetimes to repentance and faith in Christ, and so, as far as we can see, fail to attain to salvation, how is this fact of observation (and apparently of biblical testimony[8]) to be understood? Is it because God, whose will governs and determines all things, determines that it shall be so? Or is it that humans who possess 'free will' resist God's saving action and in defiance of the divine will-to-save damn themselves? The former position is associated with Calvinism and the latter with Arminianism.

Calvinism is itself a variation on the teaching of Augustine (354–430), Bishop of Hippo, who was the first to interpret the biblical evidence in a strongly 'predestinarian' direction. Beginning from the premise that salvation was entirely a gift of God,[9] and responding polemically to the teachings of the British monk Pelagius, whom he understood to be teaching that we have the capacity to save ourselves, Augustine strongly asserted the helplessness of human beings in their sin. Salvation was entirely dependent on God's eternal decision to save. Wherever the gospel is preached, some respond to it and others refuse it. This fact is explained by reference to election: God chooses to save some (the elect) but he passes by the rest and leaves them in their sins (the reprobate). The fact that he chooses some is mercy; that he leaves others in their sin is justice. It is not simply, therefore, that God foresees how people will respond: he determines what will actually come to pass and how the elect will decide.

John Calvin (1509–64), a systematic thinker and theologian of huge significance for evangelicalism, faithfully reproduced Augustine's doctrine with certain variations. Reformed theology, which springs largely from Calvin, has placed great emphasis on the 'decrees' of God, the purposes that God resolved within himself to accomplish from before the salvation of the world. Calvin modified Augustine's position by turning the concept of reprobation into an active decree. God deliberately purposes the salvation of some and the reprobation of others from before the creation of the world. Inequality of response to the preaching of the gospel is thus to be found in God's will:

> We call predestination God's eternal decree, by which he determined with Himself what He willed to become of each man. For all are not created in equal condition; rather eternal life is foreordained for some, eternal damnation for others. Therefore, as any man has been created to one or the other of these ends, we speak of him as predestined to life or death.[10]

God, therefore, is not the *watcher* of salvation, looking out for who might respond, but its *author*.[11]

It is not surprising that this severe theological system called forth some dissent. Calvin's successor in Geneva, Theodore Beza, turned out to be more of a Calvinist than Calvin. Beza, in the name of Calvin, made predestination the essence of his own theology, which has since been called 'supralapsarianism'. His system called forth a movement of opposition from within the Reformed camp itself in which the dominant voice was that of the Dutchman Jakob Arminius (1560–1609), thus giving rise to Arminianism. Those who carried forward Arminius' teaching after his death (the 'Remonstrants') set out five theses in 1610 which affirmed that:

1 God does not predestine *individuals* to life or death. Rather he predestines *classes of persons*, that is, those who believe to eternal life, and those who do not to eternal death.
2 Christ died not only for the elect but also for the whole of humankind, making it possible for all and any who believe to attain eternal life.
3 Human beings are impotent to believe apart from the Holy Spirit. (This distinguishes Arminius clearly from Pelagius.)
4 Although God's grace is the cause of salvation from beginning to end, it is not irresistible.
5 It is possible to fall from grace and be lost, and so the final perseverance of believers cannot be assumed.

In 1619 this rebellion against supralapsarian Calvinism was condemned at the Synod of Dort and gave rise to the counter-formulation of five propositions which have ever since been taken as the hallmarks of Calvinism. They are:

1 Human beings are totally depraved and so unable to redeem themselves.

2 God's grace is unconditioned by anything outside himself, so that it is not dependent on any disposition of human beings towards himself. It is sheer grace.
3 Christ died for the elect alone, since it has never been God's purpose to save the reprobate and so provision is not necessary for them.
4 God's grace is irresistible. Those whom he has chosen and calls will certainly come to repent and believe.
5 Consistent with this, it is impossible for those who are truly among the elect to lose their salvation. They will persevere in faith to the end.

It should be recognized that there are varieties of Calvinism (as with most other schools of thought) which differ in degrees of severity. *Supralapsarianism* is the most severe kind because it asserts that the decision to save some and damn others was made by God before even the decision to create the world. Creation takes place therefore as a means to the end of salvation or damnation, with the fall itself being decreed (not just permitted) by God. This really is a fatalistic perspective.

Infrapasarianism asserts that the decree to save some and reprobate others was enacted only after the decisions to create the world and to *permit* the fall. But Christ still only dies for the elect and not for the generality of humankind.

Sublapsarianism is the mildest variant and asserts that the decisions to create, permit the fall and to make atonement in Christ for the whole of humankind all preceded the decision to save or to reprobate. This can be further attenuated by returning to Augustine's view that God does not actively reprobate but simply leaves some in their self-imposed sin and alienation.

In reviewing this well-worn territory, it is hard to avoid the conclusion that the Arminians were right with their hearts and the Calvinists with their heads. The Arminian concern to see the grace of God streaming out to the whole world of humanity captures more effectively the universal love of God. The Achilles' heel of the severer brands of Calvinism seems to be the doctrine of limited or particular atonement. Of the points at which these theological systems can be tested against Scripture, this seems to be the clearest. For the New Testament unambiguously asserts the significance of Christ's death for all. He is the 'Lamb of God who takes away the sin of the world',[12] the 'atoning sacrifice for our sins and not for ours only but also for the sins of the whole world'.[13] The living God is the 'Saviour of all people, especially of those who believe'.[14] How much clearer could it be? When exegetes avoid the plain force of these texts by arguing that they refer to *all kinds of people* rather than *all people* they simply indicate that their theological system has taken over from the Bible. This in turn indicates that there is something wrong with their system.

Calvin, however, is surely right when he portrays God not as the watcher but as the author of salvation. God does not stand by to see which of all those persons to whom grace is given will find it within themselves to respond. This would still be an optimistic view of human nature. He *works* salvation. He *enables* the response so that finally we have to say that it too is a divine gift – we have nothing that we did not receive. There does seem to be an element of inequality in the way God works.

Later in this chapter I shall seek to combine these insights concerning God's universal love and his particular grace in a reconstructed statement, but not one which will answer all questions. My purpose at this point is to argue that neither traditional Calvinism nor Arminianism gives us optimistic ground on which to stand. Those who are saved are still apparently few in either system, either because 'few are chosen'[15] or because most 'judge themselves unworthy of eternal life'.[16] After all, did not Jesus, when asked whether only a few would be saved,[17] tell us to strive to enter by the *narrow* door or by the *narrow* gate for 'the road is hard that leads to life, and there are few who find it'?[18] This does seem a negative scenario and it does heighten the problem of evil. How can so much human suffering, much of it bearing no relation to sins committed, be justified when the outcome is simply eternal damnation for most? The majority of the human race ends up as nothing more than the 'waste products of the plan of salvation',[19] that which is left and discarded once the elect have been selected from the mass of perdition. And this is believed in the name of the God of love! Paradoxically it is probably Calvinism in its mild, sublapsarian form which here offers the greatest possibilities of revising this judgement. If our hope for humankind is based on the belief that human beings are perhaps not as bad as the doctrine of total depravity might suggest, that they are capable of greater response to God than we have assumed, we are deluding ourselves. If to the contrary it is rooted in the grace of God and his power to save, then it has, as I hope to show, a better foundation.

Because the situation we are left with is potentially so pessimistic, attempts have been made to soften it. This can be done by opening up a series of 'imponderables', matters to which there can be no clear answer, such as the eternal destiny of those who die in infancy, or of the mentally handicapped of whom some may be incapable, as far as we might judge, of cognitive response to God, or of the billions of humans who have never heard of Christ and his salvation because they died before he was born or have lived in cultures far removed from Christian contact. The Calvinist is able to argue that even amongst these categories God has his elect and that his election of people is unconditioned by either guilt or 'innocence'. Some 'creative accounting' might then bump up the statistics and even bring us to the point where the majority finds salvation. Such an unquestionably orthodox nineteenth-century Calvinist theologian as Charles Hodge could argue repeatedly that 'the number of the finally lost in comparison with the whole number of the saved will be very inconsiderable'.[20] Valid, and complex, though each of these matters is, and welcome as Hodge's judgement might seem, we need to begin elsewhere, and once more that starting-point is found in the trinitarian doctrine of God.

God's universal outreach

The God who is love exists independently of the world as a communion of self-giving persons in indissoluble unity. To assert that 'God is love' is not in the first instance a commentary on his relations to the world but of the exchange of love which is intrinsic to the divine being and constitutes God's infinite richness. Out from this loving, divine communion there flows the love which first creates the world and then redeems it. This dynamic, creative and then redeeming movement is to be conceived as that which proceeds from the Father through the Son and by the Spirit and then as a gathering by the Spirit through the Son back to the Father. Creation is a trinitarian activity. Creation is that divine grace whereby out of nothing the Father calls a world into being through the agency of the eternal Son[21] and in the energy of the Holy Spirit.[22] Human beings are God's good creation: basically good in that the structure of their being is God's gift, but actually *fallen* in that through self-exaltation they have alienated themselves from God and their own true destiny.

The creative activity of God is also seen in that action whereby, the world being fallen, God sets out to redeem and restore it and to bring it, despite its aberration and resistance, to its divinely intended goal. This too is a trinitarian activity as the Father sends the Son into the world in incarnation to be its re-creator, renewing and restoring the divine intention for humankind in his human existence. Because the eternal Son is the agent of creation itself, and all things have their dependence upon him, when he takes to himself a full human identity and lives and dies among us and for us, it is impossible to limit the significance of his work. The notion of a 'limited' atonement is a misjudgement. What Christ does he does for all humanity and indeed for all creation. In incarnation the eternal Word who is deemed to be the agent[23] and the sustainer[24] of all creation not only participates in human identity but in creaturehood itself, sharing in the life of the whole creation at its mineral, animal and human levels as these are recapitulated and perfected in a human being. Christ therefore has truly *universal* significance.

Through the Son, the Father also sends the Spirit. The Spirit of God is always present and is the animating Spirit within creation itself, holding it together and driving it forward towards its goal. The Spirit is also the giver of Jesus, in that the incarnation of the eternal Word, the very expression of the Father's being and nature,[25] takes place as the Word entrusts himself in self-emptying humility to the Spirit to become incarnate by that Spirit in Mary's womb and to live a human life, not of divine impregnability but of fragile human dependence upon the Spirit. The Spirit empowers and sustains Jesus of Nazareth to fulfil his messianic vocation, enables him to offer himself upon the cross[26] and then restores him to triumphant life,[27] so that he might be the first-fruits of a new creation. If the Father is the creator and the Son the re-creator, then the Spirit is the 'trans-creator', working within creation to transform it, driving and drawing it to its final consummation and the realization of its end and purpose. The Spirit is the present pledge, down payment and foretaste of the future inheritance.[28]

As the triune God is the creator of all things, so he is the restorer of all things. This is a truly universal vision because it comprehends human beings, body and soul, and all creation, visible and invisible. It also puts the apocalyptic strands of Scripture into perspective. They refer not to the fire that destroys but to that which purifies and reconstitutes, so that the present world having passed through judgement might be restored as the new heavens and new earth in which righteousness dwells.[29] Creation itself is destined not for destruction but for liberation: '[T]he creation itself will be set free from its bondage to decay and will obtain the glorious liberty of the children of God.'[30]

The popular evangelical instinct is to move quickly to the question of salvation, put crudely, to want to know who gets saved, or who goes to heaven. This represents a preoccupation with sin, to the detriment of the doctrine of creation. By restricting the work of the Spirit to the application of salvation within the Church, sight is lost of the all-encompassing presence of the Spirit within the world. Salvation is seen as removal from the world to 'heaven', rather than the return of all things to their creator in order that God may be glorified in them. This unhealthy dualism leads to the neglect of creation and embodied existence as God's gift. They are regarded as 'disposable' when in fact they are the object of salvation along with human beings. The scope of God's and the Church's mission is reduced in this way to preparing souls for heaven rather than serving the divine purpose of the restoration of all things. Creation and redemption are properly to be seen as God's dynamic, continuous action to fulfil his purpose for creation.

Rethinking election

Within this context we are able to revisit the doctrine of election and to reconceive it not as the static decision of God in a pre-temporal eternity, but as the present activity of Father, Son and Spirit to restore all things. In the formulation which follows, which is inspired by Karl Barth,[31] many of the familiar features of the doctrine of predestination will emerge, but within a different paradigm which startlingly changes their significance for the better, turning the doctrine from being bad news that sensible preachers reserve for the initiated into good news that can be proclaimed to all. Before drawing from Barth however we make some observations about the way in which the doctrine of election has usually been conceived.

Traditional discussions have neglected the fact that the doctrine of election refers to *an historical reality*, that is to say, the action of God whereby he chooses individuals and peoples in space and time to be particular agents of his work. Once removed from the biblical world-view, with its concern for historical process, and transposed into the world of philosophical discussion heavily influenced by the more abstract categories of Greek philosophy, the doctrine became concerned with *eternal decisions*, the so-called decrees of God which have occupied so much discussion and in which it was imagined that God was deciding in advance the fate of every individual. The proper arena for understanding the doctrine, however, is not eternity but history, that process whereby God works out his purpose in his own free way and does so undeniably by choosing to work through some, however unworthy they might be, and not through others, whatever claim they might advance. Classic statements such as 'I have loved Jacob, but I have hated Esau'[32] refer to the *historical fact* that Yahweh chose for his own reasons to work out his purpose through the line of Jacob. The verse does not refer to a decree before all time eternally to save Jacob or to reprobate Esau, and tells us, I suggest, absolutely nothing about the eternal fate of either. God is under no racial, cultural or personal debts but is the free Lord of history who has no obligations other than those he chooses out of grace and mercy to fulfil.

Secondly, the purpose of divine predestination is to elect peoples and persons *for a missionary task, not for exclusive privilege.* This is the point that Israel found it so hard to grasp. Israel, as all servants of God, was an agent for bringing justice and light to the nations.[33] Failure to fulfil this vocation rendered them liable to judgement. Election is a means towards wider goals and not an end in itself. It concerns universal redemption and restoration. The particularity of election must always be understood therefore as a means towards the universal realization of the divine purpose.

Thirdly, election is an *essentially personal activity*. The proper discussion is not about the philosophy of causation, about how people can be predestined and yet their decisions be still free. Nor is it about magisterial decrees promulgated in eternity and then followed through mechanically and fatalistically on earth. The doctrine of the Trinity presents us with a God who is intensely personal, not with a divine substance called 'Godhead' which makes its impact upon the world without regard to the quality of personal relations. Election is about that personal activity whereby God comes to us through Christ and in the Spirit to win us and draw us to himself. Grace is God himself in his compassionate and undeserved approach to his human creatures. To speak of grace as 'irresistible' misses this point. The approach of

Person to persons must be resistible if it is to be truly personal and relational. We can and do resist God in his grace. Indeed it is of the nature of our human fallenness that we do this. Being turned in upon ourselves we fail to respond to God either through self-sufficient pride and self-importance or by the slothfulness which cannot bring itself to make a response. The wonder of divine grace is God's persistence in seeking to win us and to overcome our resistance. Here indeed there is a mystery. It is impossible to fathom why it is that God apparently persists with some more than others and does so until he has broken their barriers down. But it is a mystery not of the Father in his inscrutable eternity, but of the Spirit who blows where he chooses[34] and whose workings are beyond our comprehension. This is an important distinction. The Father's holy love for all humanity is an open secret; the mystery is in how through the Spirit he works it out in election.

Fourthly, some attention needs to be given to the concept of *eternity*. The belief in an eternal election which reaches back to 'before the foundation of the world'[35] has come to mean for some that God has predetermined who will be saved and that nothing can change what has been decided. All that remains is to work out the unchangeable decisions of eternity in time. This concept of past eternity is questionable, since for God there is surely no past eternity but only and always the sovereign freedom over time and eternity. There are no past decisions to God but only that which is living and present. It is certainly the case that God acts and speaks out of his eternity; he does not relate to his creation as one who is static and fixed with all decisions made, but as the living and responsive God with all options open. This certainly accords with the interactive, some would say 'anthropocentric', language used of God in Scripture which portrays him as one who is open to his people, awaiting their response, taking seriously their decisions, sometimes even 'repenting' or changing his mind in response to their prayers and requests.[36] Either we take this language seriously or we do not. Astonishingly, it suggests that the eternal God has not predetermined the whole course of events but is working with events and with his people to move towards fulfilling his unchanging purpose. Put bluntly, it is still an open question what the sum total of the elect might be.

Fifthly, the discussion of predestination has tended to focus on the *will of God* rather than his *love*. By placing the emphasis on the question of whose will is supreme, that of God or of human beings, the discussion has been skewed in the direction of power rather than love and so has missed the primary point. James Orr commented on this:

> Calvin exalts the sovereignty of God and this is right. But he errs in placing his root idea of God in sovereign will rather than in love . . . I do not, therefore, abate one whit from the sovereignty of God in election, calling and salvation of such as are saved; but I do feel strongly that this election of God must not be disjoined from the context in which it is set in God's historical purpose, which, grounded in his love, embraces the widest possible ultimate blessing for the whole world. I would hold as strongly as Augustine or Calvin that only as God chooses [people] will they choose him . . . but if God's method is necessarily one of election, it is in order that in each soul saved he may set up a new centre . . . from which he may work with greater effect for the accomplishment of wider ends.[37]

With this expansive reference to the 'widest possible ultimate blessing for the whole world', the scene is set for our reconstruction.

Universal election

Here we can return to a revised paradigm for understanding election inspired in large measure by Barth. Election is first of all that decision of God in eternity to elect *himself* to be God for his people. It is his gracious turning towards the world and towards humankind of which Jesus Christ, God with us and for us, is the revelation. Supralapsarianism is correct to see that election is God's first decree, his primal decision, but wrong in identifying the content of that decree as being the inscrutable election of some and reprobation of others. There is no hidden God beyond God, no secret will which is at variance with his expressed will as though God were saying outwardly that he did not wish any to perish,[38] while secretly planning just that. The open secret about the Father, definitively revealed in Christ, is his loving will to draw us into covenant with himself. Jesus Christ, however, is not only the eternal Son come to reveal God's will for covenant. He is also the representative human being with whom God has made that covenant. Because of his eternal existence as the Word of God and his incarnation as a human being sharing by total identification in our human lot, he is uniquely qualified to represent us. He is the chosen one of God, the one who has been elected to share

God's mission, but he also represents the whole so that it becomes possible to say that the whole of humanity is chosen in him.[39] We are chosen *in Christ*.[40] This is true potentially of every human being: election is universal and no one is excluded. But it is true *actually* of those who are 'in Christ', in the sense that they have been united with him through faith, and this is the work of the Holy Spirit: election is particular. But it is particular with a view to becoming universal as the Spirit widens the circle of those who are actually elect, including them in the community which is the growing and expanding body of Christ.

Here we find the significance of Jesus' language concerning the narrow gate and the narrow road. The point about both is that only one person can pass through at a time. There is no entry *en masse* into the Kingdom of God, no slipping through because we belong to the right family, group or nation. Everyone has to go through on their own and for themselves. Personal conversion is necessary. Election must be realized in each life and is realized through the Spirit in those who believe. In this sense Christ certainly did stress the need for *individual* decision.

Christ is the elect human being. He is also the reprobate. Here we find the doctrine of 'double predestination', the belief that there is both election and reprobation, yet the object of both is Christ. He is the reprobate in the sense that he has borne our judgement and tasted in Gethsemane and at Golgotha the death and alienation which through our sins we bring upon ourselves. But if Christ is elect in order that all might be elect in him, he is made the reprobate in order that none might suffer that fate. He dies as the reprobate to deliver us. We are left with a situation therefore in which all are elect in Christ and none need be lost. This is good news. This can be proclaimed.

Election and universalism

Does this formulation leave us, however, with an inevitable universalism which means that all *will* be saved? Here we need to distinguish between different kinds of 'universalism'. If by that term we mean that God loves the whole world, everyone and everything in it, that his purposes are universal and move towards the restoration of all things to himself,[41] that Christ has died for every person and each one may be hoped for, then everything that we have argued in this chapter disposes us to say 'absolutely so'! Such a position I take to be the message of the Scriptures. But if by 'universalism' is meant the *inevitability* that all will finally attain salvation, this would be to turn a universal hope into a dogmatic certainty, something which can only be done by ignoring integral parts of the biblical witness. At this point the strain of negativity within evangelicalism, which I have argued threatens to become excessive, is a vital witness to the possibility of the tragic. Eternal loss is a real possibility. To eradicate this devalues the significance of human decision. There are real decisions to be made with real and eternal consequences. To deny this would be like claiming that people are drowning, but only in two inches of water. There is real risk which justifies the real warnings, and dogmatic universalism devalues the seriousness of human life, decision and history by avoiding it.

Human beings have the capacity to resist divine grace and possibly even to resist it finally. If there is hope it is not based upon a belief that they will choose to make the right decisions, but on the grace of God. We have noted the realism in the teaching of Jesus concerning human beings. Yet that realism was balanced by hope in God. When Jesus spoke about how hard it was for those with riches to enter the Kingdom of God, the disciples questioned, 'Then who can be saved?' Jesus replied that 'for God all things are possible'.[42] God's omnipotent grace is the reality with which we have to reckon, and God's will-to-save is made known in Christ. A 'hopeful universalism' which neither counts upon the salvation of all nor rules out the possibility that all may finally be saved is a theological possibility. But it involves the tension of living faithfully within the magnetic field set up by the amazing grace of God and the appalling sin of the world.[43] We can set limits neither to the grace of God nor to his justice.

Maximum hope

My contention is that the kind of trinitarian theology of creation and redemption I have outlined is an antidote to excessive negativity without attenuating the necessary realism concerning human nature that evangelicalism has traditionally maintained. It enables us to regard the whole world of humanity not as Christians or non-Christians, elect or reprobate, but as those in whom election has been realized and those in whom it has yet to be realized. There are Christians and 'not-yet-Christians',

Christians in fact and 'designated Christians' or 'Christians in hope'.[44] This is a healthy foundation on which to engage in Christian mission. The position I have outlined raises further questions that we do not have space here to address. Amongst these is the rather unevangelical issue of 'the larger hope', the suggestion that the physical death of the human is not itself for all people the ultimate boundary beyond which it becomes impossible to find redemption. There is a salvation that reaches beyond death. To this issue we shall return in chapter 7.

4

Scripture: Freedom and Limit

Evangelicals are Bible-believing people and make it their duty to hold fast to the Scriptures and to defend their authority. All of this I wish to affirm. The question is whether the secondary claim that evangelicals must therefore be committed to a particular set of judgements about the Bible is justified. Among evangelicals a variety of opinions can be found concerning the *formal* nature of biblical authority and in what precisely it consists. But even those who agree concerning a doctrine of Scripture might diverge widely over the *material* nature of its authority and what it actually teaches on any given topic, and even more about the *significance* of that teaching for the world of today. Believing in the Bible turns out to be more complex than might at first be imagined.

Scripture alone?

One of the watchwords of the Reformation proclaimed *sola scriptura*, that the Scriptures alone are the Church's teaching authority. This claim was, in the circumstances, understandable and necessary. The sources of Christian faith in the teaching of Christ and the apostles had become overlaid by centuries of Church tradition. The Reformers were therefore engaged in a mission of recovery, restoring the Bible to its rightful place and allowing it to speak directly and cogently to Church and world. Yet, on reflection, is it ever possible to have the Bible *alone*? Is not any text only ever understood through complex processes involving other texts and diverse forces which shape and determine what we read and how we understand it? Although the Bible may be the *supreme* authority for the Church, lesser authorities are also inevitably shaping the way it is understood and applied.

People do not, after all, come to the Bible free from presuppositions. Whatever the claims for the logical priority of Scripture, psychologically we usually begin elsewhere. From the first moment of contact with a faith-community we are being socialized and instructed into its tradition and are reading the Bible in the light of it. The tradition can highlight for us what is of greatest significance. The biblical canon is so extensive that it is possible to overlook or minimize certain strands within it: the Bible is then read in a way determined in advance by the tradition from which we come. In this sense the evangelical runs the same risks of traditionalism as any other kind of Christian. She or he risks investing that tradition with divine authority in the belief that it is an unquestionable reflection of the biblical teaching. Evangelicalism often domesticates the Bible to make it justify its own concerns as in, for instance, the constant tendency to apply it to the personal and inner world to the neglect of the social and political.

The Bible can also only be understood as we apply our rational minds to it. Historically, evangelicalism has taken this task very seriously. Yet here too we need to be aware of the authority of reason. Rationality is a social construct and different social groups reason differently. The very way Westerners think is shaped by the intellectual history of their culture, and a 'pure' reading of the Bible is a sheer impossibility. Every reading is a contextual reading. Once this is understood it becomes clearer that fundamentalism, which makes the claim to be faithful to the Bible in opposition to modern culture, is itself very much a product of that culture. By insisting that the Bible is at all points a book of 'facts', it shows itself to be a typical product of the scientific, empirical world-view.[1] The Bible becomes objectified, homogenized and literalized by such an approach.

Rationality is authoritative and must be taken seriously. But we have said enough to indicate that patterns of rationality shift. What is plausible to one generation ceases to be so to the next, for instance the occurrence of 'supernatural' acts of God. When we read the Bible, we carry our own particular cultural baggage with us and it shapes what we find. This is inevitable and in its own way potentially enriching. Interaction with our culture and close attendance to its questions and perspectives can enable us to grasp how previous readings of the Bible have been culturally bound and have prevented us from seeing and hearing what has been there all along, for instance the liberating words it speaks about the dignity of women, or charismatic gifts. In this sense, a proper reading of Scripture is dependent upon the willingness to listen to the world as well as to the Word. But in this process the Word must have the last word.

There is a further way in which social context exercises authority. Everyone reads the Bible with a view to their own self-interest. We are glad to find in the authoritative book that which legitimates our own power, privilege or wealth (if we possess them) and prejudices (which we certainly do), because it enables us to believe that the way things are for us is the way God wants them to be. Christian slave owners once justified their position by reference to Scripture. Many white Afrikaaners in South Africa believed for a time that the apartheid system could be given biblical support. Some North Americans justify the culture of material aspiration by reference to the biblical promises of prosperity. There are few who use the Bible *against* themselves and their own interests in self-criticism. This constant danger helps us to appreciate the claim of the liberation theologians that the true meaning of the Bible is most likely to be understood not by the powerful and privileged but by the poor for whom God has a particular concern. This 'hermeneutical privilege' requires the whole Church to read and understand the Bible from the perspective of the poor and powerless and to be critical of any reading which neglects this element.

Scripture is never 'alone'. Other forces always shape our understanding. Our interpretation of biblical revelation never reaches its final point in this life. God has spoken decisively to us in Christ and this revelation stands over against us, but our grasp of it is capable of improvement,[2] as with any branch of human enquiry. The witness of Scripture to Christ is supreme and acts as the canon for all claims to theological authority. Yet all of us are cast in the role of pilgrims, seeking to live under the authority of divine revelation as we confidently yet modestly journey towards the time of 'knowing as we have been known'. Relative human beings must never confuse their relative constructs with the absolute itself.

Scripture: form and content

Much evangelical debate about the Bible has focused disproportionately upon the form of Scripture, to the detriment of its content. The passage which makes the most explicit claim to the divine inspiration of Scripture makes no deductions about what this implies for the form of Scripture but rather emphasizes its purpose. Because Scripture is inspired by God it is *'useful* for teaching, for reproof, for correction and for training in right-eousness'.[3] Being responsive to what the Bible teaches is more important than possessing the correct views about it. This by no means renders debates about its form irrelevant, but it does place them in proper perspective.

The approach which I here espouse assesses the Bible accord-ing to its primary function of bearing witness to God and his acts of creating and redeeming humankind, acts which find fulfilment in the career of Jesus Christ. Evangelicals have been right to insist that because God's activity is *historical* the Bible must be under-stood as reliable testimony to those divine acts, offering divinely inspired interpretation of what they mean. The Bible is best understood as a 'cumulative process of events and their interpre-tation'.[4] God is active in history and by the inspiration of the Spirit the witnesses to those acts have perceived their meaning and borne their testimony. Yet, as part of a cumulative process, those acts have been seen time and again to accumulate fresh significance and have contributed to the understanding of new acts of God. Undoubtedly therefore there is in the Bible a process of development, and whereas each stage is significant in itself, its overall meaning is only properly understood within the context of the whole. It is apt to liken the Bible to an ancient cathedral which has built upon and taken up into the final structure fragments of previous buildings on the same site. The style of individual parts may reflect ages long past and may fit awkwardly into the whole, but they have their unique place in a unique whole and make their contribution even as they are surpassed by the final construction.

The evangelical insistence that if Scripture is indeed to be profitable and to fulfil its function it must bear reliable and truth-ful witness to history, constitutes the strength of that position. Dismissive criticism which denies the historical core of the Bible will be regarded as destructive of Christian faith, and rightly so. However, the emphasis upon reliable witness to divine historical acts helps us to distinguish between what it is necessary to defend concerning the Bible and what not.

a. *The Bible and cosmology*

It is not necessary, for instance, to defend a particular cosmology. Prior to the scientific revolutions of Galileo and Copernicus it was natural to assume that the universe was constructed in the way in which humans themselves experienced it. From the human perspective the sun and moon revolved around the earth and there was no reason to assume that the world was anything other than flat. The alterations of perspective made possible by the telescope brought into question the common experience of human beings and showed that a true understanding of the world is quite other than that which had long been assumed.

The Bible more or less shares the ancient, 'common sense' cosmology. The scientific revolution therefore posed questions about biblical interpretation. Certain biblical statements could no longer be taken as literally or 'scientifically' true, but true in the sense that they were true to human experience. Although the Bible reflects an ancient cosmology, it is not the purpose of the Bible to *teach* such a cosmology, but to bear witness to the saving acts of God within a context where that cosmology was generally believed. Here is a case in point where engagement with the wider human intellectual endeavour is necessary for a proper understanding of the Bible, enabling us to discriminate between what is essential and what is peripheral to its intent. Those conservatives who in the name of faithfulness to Scripture hold to a 'literal' interpretation of the seven days of creation miss the point about the purpose of the Bible. The point is to discover how making use of the language and intellectual equipment of their day they bear their testimony to God and his saving actions. To extend the authority of the Bible to make it speak to issues which go well beyond its primary intention is to misuse it and creates unnecessary obstacles to faith.

To treat the Bible as a textbook on all matters is to go beyond the limits of its function; yet this needs to be qualified by the assertion that the witness of Scripture gives rise to convictions about God and the way he deals with the world, which will certainly affect the way we view the whole world. Theological thinking can and should be brought to bear on all things, and no doubt has many puzzles with which to wrestle, but it will not accomplish this by a text-proofing approach to the Bible in itself but by a more complex process of theological thought.

b. *The Bible and history*

If the understanding we are developing frees us from the need to embrace outmoded cosmologies (and even current cosmologies will in due course become outmoded), it may also free us from the monolithic view of Scripture frequently found among conservative evangelicals. For to claim that Scripture bears witness reliably to God's historical acts is not to say that everything in it counts as literal history. It is clearly the case that the Christian faith depends upon certain events of history and collapses if those events can be shown to be illusory. This is centrally true of the cross and resurrection of Christ. If Christ did not live and die, then the Christian story of salvation is untrue. If Christ has not risen from death, then Christian proclamation is utterly in vain.[5] Yet this does not mean that all the apparent events recorded in the Bible share an equal status. The truth of Jesus' parables is in no way dependent upon a certain man actually going down from Jerusalem to Jericho and falling among robbers as a matter of literal history,[6] although no doubt similar things happened. Stories, even ones which never actually happened, can be effective vehicles of truth. It is possible to speak of historical realities by means of many literary genres, and it is a wooden form of logic that argues that if Scripture is shown to be non-historical or non-factual at one point, then it cannot be received as reliable history at any point. This monolithic view, that Scripture is literal history at all points, surely overlooks the variety and depth of human speech in general, and of biblical testimony in particular. God has spoken to us in 'many and varied ways' and supremely in a living human being.[7] The point is, and many seem to find it difficult to grasp, that history may be spoken of through media which are not themselves literal history. Here we give some random examples simply to illustrate the point.

Genesis 2 and 3 record the creation and fall of human beings. Adam and Eve are created by God and fall from communion with him in the Garden of Eden when they are tempted by the serpent and disobey God's command by eating of the fruit which was forbidden them. As a consequence they are driven from the garden and precipitate the race into disaster. For many evangelicals the literal acceptance of this narrative is foundational to the whole of Scripture, not least because the Apostle Paul refers to it as an historical entry-point of sin and death.[8] Karl Barth once called the advocates of such literalism 'the friends of the speaking serpent'.

The domino and 'thin-end-of-the-wedge' theories suggest that if we accept this narrative as not literally true we must give up on the rest of the Bible on the premise of 'wrong at one point, wrong at all points'. Yet something may be true without being *literally* true, since there are different vehicles of truth. Many of the figures of speech we employ are *literally* untrue but nonetheless adequate vehicles of truthful communication. A portrait of a person is not as accurate as a photograph but may actually capture depths to a person more truthfully than a camera ever could. Truth can be expressed through symbol, poetry and legend. Even the category 'myth' can be employed if it is understood not, as is popularly the case, as something which is untrue but as the true description of reality in the form of a symbolic narrative. The simplest and least problematic way of understanding the Eden narrative is as a symbolic description of an historical reality. What it describes is historical in the sense that human beings of all generations are fallen. But there must also have been those first human beings who first did what we all do, namely fall away from God in primal and wilful disobedience. So sin and spiritual death entered in. The important truth about the narrative is that it describes 'Adam', whose name means humankind, and in a way destined to seize the imagination of people across hugely different cultures and at many different times; it lays bare the truth about our alienated and tragic existence. It is a symbolic way of speaking of historical realities.

A further example of the way in which biblical material presents and interprets historical realities through non-literal media is the book of Jonah. To scour the annals of seafarers, as sometimes happens, for 'big fish' stories proving that human beings can survive in the bellies of sea creatures[9] is to miss the point altogether. The book of Jonah is most likely to be an allegory and the historical realities it interprets concern the experience of the Jewish people in the exile in Babylon and subsequent restoration to their own land.[10] Understood in this sense it remains very much a book about history, opening up and disclosing the inner meaning of those crisis events. Like Jonah, the Jewish people sought to escape their prophetic vocation to the unbelieving nations. As a consequence they were judged by being swallowed up by the Babylonian empire. In exile they came, as did Jonah in the fish, to a place of repentance and renewal. They were returned to their land for a surprising and undeserved second opportunity to succeed, and the prophetic call was renewed. It is irrelevant to enquire whether the story of Jonah literally 'happened'. But the events which it interprets certainly did. To argue for the literal historicity of this book on the ground that Jesus, in connection with the resurrection, referred to Jonah's being 'three days and three nights in the belly of the sea monster',[11] mistakes the fact that Jesus is drawing upon the literary heritage of his people to make his point rather than confirming its 'factual' status.

We could go on developing examples. The point we are making is that there is an essentially historical core to the biblical tradition but that the meaning and significance of that history is opened up to us through parables, sagas, poetry, allegories, symbols, prophecies, apocalyptic and even (when we understand the word properly) myth. It is to misuse the Bible to insist that this many-textured body of literature can only be understood in one way – as literal, factual history at every point. This approach imposes upon the Bible a set of expectations which are inappropriate and have narrowed down the understanding of 'truth' to a scientific model of one-to-one correspondence. A more reverent approach would be to accept the Bible on its own terms for what it is – an ancient book which was hundreds of years in its development and which bears the traces of the cultural milieux and assumptions from which it has arisen. It reflects their criteria, not ours. With the language of its own day and times it bears its witness to the saving actions of God. It is not up to us to set in advance the terms on which that revelation could come to us, but to accept it the way it is.

The issue of 'inerrancy'

Our ability to appreciate the Bible is not assisted by the concept of 'inerrancy', by means of which some evangelicals would like to determine who is or is not a 'proper' evangelical. It is a feature of the evangelical coalition that, lacking an authoritative teaching magisterium and depending instead upon consensus, it gives excessive attention to a cluster of secondary issues as a way of maintaining boundaries for its identity.[12] The concept of inerrancy, the claim that the Bible is free from all kinds of error, is one such. Yet once it is accepted that the Bible contains many kinds of literature, functioning according to varying assumptions, it becomes complicated to define satisfactorily in what sense those forms are 'inerrant' or without error. Much human speech is in error on one level and true on another, depending on the way the conventions of language are understood and the intentions of the user are framed. Some evangelicals have wanted to insist, for example, that no 'pseudonymous' literature (written *in the name* of a person who did not in fact write it or write the whole of it, as for instance Proverbs[13] and arguably 2 Peter[14]) is found in Scripture, on the grounds that this would both be erroneous and a form of deception. But much literature is written in an assumed identity, and because this is generally known and understood it counts as a convention rather than a deception. If in the world in which these biblical books were written this convention of pseudonymity was understood and appreciated there seems no reason why it should not be employed as a vehicle of truth or why we from our lofty vantage-point should decree otherwise. In Scripture, God accommodates himself to our human conditions.

The paradox is that everybody, bar a few on the very extremes, actually believes that the Bible we possess and use, and which in fact proves to be the means of God's Word being addressed to us, does contain errors. Inerrancy is usually attributed only to the manuscripts 'as originally given' yet which have long since been lost. We possess a multitude of copies from which the originals can be reconstructed with remarkable accuracy, but cannot pretend that we have access to an inerrant text. The Bible nonetheless fulfils its crucial task despite the imperfections of the versions we possess. Logically the idea of inerrancy derives from a standard evangelical approach to inspiration, according to which, because the Scriptures are 'breathed-out' by God, they must partake of the properties of the divine nature, one of which is that God is never in error.[15] Yet this formulation neglects the implications of the fact that the biblical witness is refracted through human channels employing regular speech which participates in the limitations of finitude. It errs on the divine side of Scripture rather than the human, where what is required is a proper balance and an awareness of the divine ability (and will) in grace to take up and use imperfect instruments. It is preferable to see inspiration as that divine activity whereby God enables the biblical writers to make their witness to himself and his saving actions. It is not necessary for them in this to be inerrant concerning everything on which they speak but to be *reliable* in giving their witness as people of their own day and age, sufficiently reliable to fulfil the primary purpose of Scripture which is 'to instruct you for salvation through faith in Jesus Christ'.[16]

To speak in positive terms of the *reliability* and *sufficiency* of Scripture is preferable to the ultimately indefinable language of inerrancy. When properly approached and understood, the Bible does not lead astray but fulfils its purpose of leading to Christ with divine power and energy. In that some evangelicals seem to hold on to the word 'inerrancy' symbolically as a hedge against negative attitudes, to denote the value of the Bible and to affirm that it should be listened to with extreme attention, their intention can be appreciated. But the word 'inerrancy' is then retained more for its symbolic rather than its cognitive content.[17]

Living with and under the Word of God

A radical evangelical approach to the Bible accepts its normative and definitive witness to Christ without feeling obliged to overstate the implications of this for its form. The Bible can be accepted as a fully human collection of writings, to be studied as such, but also as divinely inspired since it is of the nature of God's action as revealed in the incarnation that God imparts himself through assuming the human and not by-passing it.

God's Spirit has inspired the writers to make their witness, and that same Spirit can enlighten those who read what they wrote. None of us possesses a final interpretation of this. We are in pilgrimage. But not to know everything is not to know nothing. We know *in part* but we also *know* in part. We turn our attention here to the matter rather than the form of Scripture. What ultimately counts is what is said and how we are responding to it.

Wrestling with the Bible

The Bible is not a flat textbook, all of whose parts are of equal significance and from which texts might be pieced together to produce a systematic theology. Such an approach engages the brain and the ingenuity but not much else. Instead we should view the Bible as a world of discourse which engages us totally and which we are called to indwell in order to understand. The revelation of God witnessed in Scripture does not develop in a smooth and straightforward way with all parts conveniently harmonious. Instead it develops *dialectically* with true but partial understandings of God being expanded, sometimes questioned, by new acts and new insights into God's ways. The Bible invites us to enter into its world, to appreciate the affirmations it makes and the questions it poses, to follow the process whereby the existing knowledge of God is checked and expanded by new events and their interpretations. God's Word emerges through this as a rising trajectory which is fulfilled in Christ himself. Its aim is not to grant us knowledge *about* God alone but to nourish within us the knowledge of God *himself*, who is always greater and more mysterious than any single word or cluster of statements might suggest. Centrally, Scripture leads us up to Christ who as the Word made flesh is the culmination in history of divine revelation and from whom all subsequent Christian reflection on God must proceed. The honest reader of the Bible will therefore be engaged in an uncomfortable process which at times thrills, encourages and overawes but alternatively also offends, scandalizes, puzzles, angers and mystifies.

The Bible simply is not the kind of book that right-thinking religious moderns would choose as their sacred literature. It is hopelessly politically incorrect. But through the gamut of emotions it awakens, we are in fact being engaged at depth in an experience that has the potential to be life-transforming. Through it we are following the ways of God as he has been progressively perceived in response to his gracious initiative. Supremely, we are being led to Christ as that one in whom both God is revealed and the proper nature of our response to that God is made known. We grasp the function and power of the Bible correctly when we see it as the primary instrument to enable us to live under the authority and in the light of the one of whom it speaks.

The Bible as story

The notion that the Bible conveys to us a drama and invites us to enter into its continuing flow has been developed to good effect by Tom Wright.[18] The Bible's authority does not consist in the fact that it offers us timeless truths. Rather it enables us to submit ourselves to the authority of God which is made known through Jesus and the Spirit, and has the character of loving, creative, redeeming wisdom. Its authority is that of a story and can be understood by means of an analogy with a Shakespearian play in five acts of which the final act has yet to be written. The decision is made to allow a cast of skilled actors, well acquainted with Shakespeare, to improvise the fifth act. To do this they must immerse themselves in the first four acts of the drama which are known, coming to appreciate intimately the characterizations of the story, its background and plot, and so entering into the mind and intention of the author. The first four acts are therefore the 'authority' for what the actors are to do and the improvisation must maintain continuity with these acts. This can be tested because it may be objected that any given aspect of improvisation departs from what is commonly known from the first four acts. There is need therefore for both consistency and improvisation, and the actors are themselves dependent upon a degree of inspiration for the task they are given, inspiration which arises from the first four acts but which goes beyond this to what they perceive the mind and intention of the author to be. Their improvisation could not consist in merely repeating what was contained in the first four acts but must move to complete the intention of the drama by responsibly entering into the narrative and carrying it forward.

Wright's analogy with Scripture suggests that the five acts of the biblical drama are creation, fall, Israel, and Jesus, with the rest of the New Testament constituting the first scene of the final act and with hints as to how the play is supposed to end. The Church lives under the 'authority' of the story as it is extant, but is required both to improvise and to perform the remainder of the final act.

Whatever its limitations, Wright's suggestion does capture some of the vital elements of Christian existence under the Word as we experience it. The Christian calling is so to live and act as to further the purposes of God's Kingdom. To do this effectively it is necessary to understand the nature of the God we serve and his purposes. Such knowledge is not acquired mechanically by manipulating a text, but in a costly fashion which involves entering sympathetically into God's story as we possess it. To do this, no part of the story should be neglected since although certain parts are crucial to the narrative and set out the author's intention with added clarity, even the parts of the drama deemed to have lesser significance contribute to the total impact of the play or to its background. As the author's intention becomes more clearly understood, even opaque aspects of the drama come more clearly into focus. To reject parts of the story because the individual actor finds them uncongenial or to attempt to rewrite or write in different terms what has been given is to deny the integrity of the task and end up with an infinitely poorer version of the drama.

Nor does this story impose itself upon us coercively since it is not the nature of stories to coerce and impose, but to liberate, inspire, illuminate and invite. The process requires total engagement as we attend to the ways of God made known and follow the course of the story with particular attention to the career of Jesus in which the decisive clues and insights as to its meaning are disclosed in clearest measure. Through this we are involved in a process of formation whereby we become the kind of persons who are able to extend the drama. There is no loss of freedom as though life under the Word deprives us of options and alternatives, indeed such submission frees us for responsibility. There is wonder and amazement at the creativity and passion of what has been written, evoking the response of love. There is a responsible weighing of which actions and directions are consonant with the story made known and carry it further. The intellect and heart are engaged, since the call is to enter into the mind and intention of the author. We need to draw upon the best resources of reflection, tradition and interpretation to be sure that we have understood this mind to the best of our ability.

Yet there is not necessarily only one way of carrying the story forward and attaining the desired goal: there may be many ways of improvising and we make our free and creative contribution to this. The Spirit who inspired the first acts continues to inspire those who attend to them diligently, so that inspiration is not only an affirmation concerning how the biblical literature was formed but also about our reception of it. The process of interpretation takes place corporately as understandings of the drama are enriched and tested through other readings of the text. Finally, there is no guarantee that in taking forward the drama we are able to do so faultlessly or without deviations, but the existing Word, the Spirit and the community of interpreters assist us in obviating or mitigating actions discontinuous with the first acts of the drama.

The Bible as liberating wisdom

A full exposition of the doctrine of Scripture requires far more reflection than we here have space to devote to it. I have sought to set out an approach to the Bible which takes with full seriousness its inspiration and authority and which requires us to focus on its content. It is not correct beliefs about the Bible which have priority but living engagement with it so that God's Word may be addressed to us. I have shown how the historical nature of revelation can be taken seriously without lapsing into literalism or insisting that the Bible fulfil literary expectations which belong to our age, not its own. The Bible is not ultimately to be read as a law book (although it contains varieties of law) but as wisdom which liberates. The highest manifestation of that divine wisdom is the central figure of the Christian interpretation of Scripture, Jesus Christ, who is for us 'wisdom from God, and righteousness and sanctification and redemption'.[19] We are invited to share in Christ, to learn his wisdom and to be wise in our own generation.

5

The Creative Redeemer

Evangelicalism has characteristically embraced the theme of redemption to the detriment of the doctrine of creation. Indeed, the contemplation of redemption has, according to Mark Noll, at times almost totally replaced respect for creation.[1] As a consequence, evangelicals have often produced people who know how to analyse and denounce what is wrong with the world but are less adept at celebrating it as a gracious gift from God, or at conceiving creation as a whole as the object of redemption. There are, of course, many exceptions but both the friends and the critics of evangelical faith will recognize a substantial grain of truth in this and in the habits of mind to which it points. At its worst extremes these can border on the Manichaean, regarding anything outside the Church and Christianity as but the practice of error.[2] A theological antidote to this pathology, which is not confined to evangelicalism, is at hand in the trinitarian theology we have already affirmed. The whole world is the creation and gift of the Father, through the Son, by the Spirit, fallen but still structurally good.

In this chapter we focus upon evangelical approaches to redemption and atonement. Evangelical 'crucicentrism', while in principle entirely right, can dispose the movement to exalt redemption at the expense of creation. Creation is taken for granted, redemption is what is required. My intention is not to dispense with the centrality of the cross but to question whether evangelical understandings of it have been either sufficiently broad or adequately profound and so have obscured as well as highlighted the truth that we need to understand.

Evangelicals and penal substitution

If it is true, as we claimed in chapter 4, that evangelical identity is protected by exalting certain second-order doctrines to first-order status, then the doctrine of penal substitution is one such, to be ranked in importance with inerrancy. This belief considers that Christ has borne the wrath of God upon the cross, being punished by the Father in place of sinful human beings. On Christ has been laid a weight of sin which is equivalent to the judgement that we deserve. Because he has borne our burden in our place we can be acquitted.

This formulation of atonement has been powerful not least because it offers a simple way of grasping a reality, atonement, which is difficult to state. It has strengths that we shall certainly wish to retain. Yet it is a high-risk formulation, in that it readily lends itself to caricature. As the offence of the cross is made much of in the New Testament,[3] it is essential to be clear about what is the real offence and what is merely crude theology.

Penal substitution, for example, risks presenting a loving Son appeasing a wrathful and angry Father. This is not the intention of the New Testament which clearly asserts the origin of the cross in the love of the Father. Neither has it been the intention of the best proponents of the doctrine. But the caricature lies close to hand. Further, the image of a father punishing a son for an offence he has not committed is morally dubious. John Stott is entirely right to stress that the only kind of substitution which can avoid this taint is that of *divine self-substitution*, in which God himself endures the cost of human forgiveness.[4] This is precisely what the doctrines of Trinity and incarnation enable us to affirm.

There are clues here to a deeper theological understanding of substitution which are extremely welcome, yet it is only with great care that they can be elucidated and the caricatures avoided. In what follows we shall argue for a reconstructed doctrine of atonement which draws upon a wider range of images to expound what has taken place through the cross for our reconciliation.

Metaphors of atonement

It is commonplace when discussing atonement to distinguish between the *fact* of atonement which is apprehended in faith and the *theories* by which that fact is elucidated.[5] The theories never adequately express the reality. Theories of atonement are metaphors by means of which the height and depth of atonement and reconciliation are explored. Each generation of theological thinkers tends to interpret the atonement through metaphors which relate it to their own day and context and in doing so retrieve elements of the remarkably rich New Testament witness which previous generations may have ignored.

For instance, the thinkers of the sub-apostolic and patristic periods focused upon the atoning work of Christ in its impact upon human beings and the powers of evil. Christ's work was perceived in the first instance as a work of spiritual enlightenment, of participation in the divine nature, or of example. In this sense the cross was not the single aspect of atonement to be explored. Rather, the death of Christ was subordinate to his saving birth, life and resurrection. Christ was perceived as the teacher or heavenly tutor who could enlighten all who believed. The physical assumption of human nature by God in the incarnation was, in the Eastern understanding of salvation, the means whereby human beings could participate in God and so attain to eternal life. In this understanding, Christ undergoes death in order to transform and overcome it, to emerge from it triumphantly in resurrection, in a way which then allows him to be the life-giving mediator for those who participate in him through grace. The foundations of the Eucharist as a means of physically participating in Christ can here be seen. In addition, in his total manner of life, Christ elicits from human beings a response of faith which causes them to follow his example and conform their lives to him in a morally transforming fashion. Salvation is very much, therefore, the product of the life of Christ. This approach to Christ's saving work does not yet say a great deal about the cross, but captures dimensions which evangelicalism has been in danger of ignoring. The saving work of Christ is the outcome of his total career and though it may be focused peculiarly in the cross this should not eclipse its full scope.

In patristic doctrine, a theology of the cross developed around the concept of the death of Christ as a ransom payment.[6] If a ransom is a payment made in order to set someone free, the question follows, 'To whom was the ransom paid?' One patristic answer was that Christ's death was the payment made to the devil, who held the race in bondage, as the price for setting humankind free. This choice of options had fateful consequences. Atonement theory developed along the lines of a bargain between God and the devil, whereby as the price for liberating human captives the devil required the soul of Christ. So Christ enters into death through the cross, but, having gained human freedom, is raised by God from death to triumph over the devil.

Even carefully stated, this makes the atonement sound like a trick or even a deception perpetrated by God on the devil. As this trick was elaborated by the means of ever grosser imagery, the ransom theory came into disrepute. Yet this 'classical theory' of the atonement has more recently undergone a revival. Indeed, underlying it are some biblical and theologically significant themes. It is right to view the work of Christ as a work of liberation. This is implied in the very notion of redemption. Slaves are liberated from their bondage at a cost. Gustav Aulen developed the significance of this imagery and expounded the work of Christ as a continuous act of God whereby he overcomes the powers of death, wrath, law, guilt and the devil.[7] Although we might well have problems with the patristic notion that the devil has rights and can strike bargains with God, the deeper significance of this imagery is that when God brings redemption about he does so justly and in a way which satisfies all legitimate demands.

There is theological depth to the notion that evil has a tendency to overreach itself, that it destroys itself by means of its own inherent contradictions. Talk of the devil needs some exposition in the modern world, yet the language of the demonic has again in this century proved its worth as a manner of speaking of evil forces which achieve a dynamic of their own over and above the individual acts of people. Through refusing to submit to it even at the cost of his own death, Christ has overcome a world system which resists God. He then invites us, in communion with himself, to do the same. In reformulation, the ransom theory has great potential in an age when the theme of liberation and freedom resonates with so much of our experience.

A sacrifice to God

The grosser ways in which the ransom theory found expression prepared the way for a shift of perception which gave renewed attention to the atonement as a price paid to God rather than to the devil. Evangelicalism stands firmly in this tradition. The cross is a sacrifice, an offering to God that transforms the situation of human beings. The Old Testament contains prescriptions for many different forms of sacrifice to enact a range of religious emotions. At the centre of this complex edifice was the Day of Atonement on which the High Priest was to enter the Holy of Holies in the tabernacle, and later the temple, with the blood of sacrifice in atonement for the sins of the people.[8] There appear to be two ways in which the *efficacy* of sacrifice could be conceived: older assumptions were that sacrifice enacted a transfer of divine wrath away from the sinner and onto the sacrificial victim who was punished in the sinner's place. An alternative interpretation is that the blood of a sacrificial victim represents the *release of life* in such a way as to renew or purify a life which has been sullied by sin. The blood of the sacrifice therefore acts as a powerful cleansing agent purifying the polluting effect of human sin. In the first instance, the victim passively bears a punishment not its own; in the second, the offering of the sacrifice is proactive. Both are concerned with divine wrath, but the former sees the wrath of God being removed through propitiation as it is endured by a substitute; in the second, divine wrath is removed because the *causes* of that wrath in human sin are taken away or expiated.

Anselm (1033–1109), Archbishop of Canterbury, was the major influence in the shift away from a theology of atonement as a payment made to the devil towards a theology of 'satisfaction'.[9] Christ made an offering to God which satisfied the divine honour. Here there are echoes of the second, proactive approach to sacrifice we identified. Anselm was drawing upon the feudal context which located order and stability in the person of the overlord. To offend this person was to jeopardize one's position and invite punishment. God is conceived then as a feudal lord whose honour is the guarantee of social stability. In that human beings have failed to give to God what is his due, they have sinned against him. To restore to God his honour they must either make amends for what they have done or God must vindicate his own honour through punishment. As they are incapable of making amends, and as to punish humankind with death would mean that God's purposes could not be fulfilled, God's Son has become incarnate in order that from within the human race and on its behalf he might do for them what they could not do for themselves. For atonement must be made by a human being for human beings. Yet atonement can only actually be made by God, since humans are incapable of the act. The outcome is that Christ, the 'God-Man' makes atonement in a way which is both the gift of God and a fully human act. But as a human being, Christ also owes to God everything he has and is. To make amends for the race he must bring to God something that he does not already owe to God. That gift is the offering of his own death which, as a sinless person, he does not owe, and this offering is sufficient to restore God's honour and make atonement on behalf of all. Christ therefore makes active atonement to God in such a way as to compensate for human beings and to remove the pollution of their sin.

Anselm's account of atonement quickly gained acceptance because of the intellectual force with which it was expressed. He set out to provide a rational account of the necessity of God's becoming a human being and did so compellingly. There are, of course, elements lacking from his account which critics are not slow to identify. Chiefly, the picture of the divine feudal overlord who is concerned for his own honour fails to capture the heart of atonement in the New Testament, which is the passionate love of God for his sinful creatures. The introduction of the satisfaction motif into atonement theory shifts the focus to what the cross implies for God himself. Its danger is in conveying the impression that atonement happens for God's sake rather than ours, as the means whereby he makes it possible for himself to forgive.

Anselm also bequeathed to those who came after him the inclination to conceive of sin as a debt or a weight which we carry. Sin and guilt are conceived externally and quantitatively, as a burden to be shed or a debt to be paid, rather than internally and qualitatively as a disorder to be put right or a sickness to be healed. However, any person's work should always be judged against the benchmark of what they set out to achieve, and by this standard Anselm's work is a landmark in theology generally and in reflection on the atonement in particular.

Penal substitution

Anselm's shift of interpretation in a God-ward direction prepared the ground for the Reformers, and especially Calvin, to develop the doctrine of penal substitution. In doing so they were retrieving the biblical teaching concerning the wrath of God.[10] The satisfaction due to God did not, for Calvin, primarily concern the divine honour but the divine wrath. Unlike Anselm's approach which saw atonement for sin and punishment as alternatives, such that

God would only punish human beings if they failed to make amends and so satisfy his honour, for the Reformers atonement was achieved *through* the inflicting of punishment. In this they were reflecting their own context in which early democratic thinking was developing and the law was no longer identified with the person of the ruler. Rulers were now themselves subject to a higher law, to be applied equally to all, as Charles I was later to find out. The law had to be vindicated and was vindicated through the imposition of punishment. Clearly, for human beings to be punished for their sin would destroy them and so it was believed that atonement was accomplished through Christ taking the place of sinners and being punished in their place. This doctrine, which is relatively easy to grasp, has predominated within evangelicalism, sometimes to the exclusion of other approaches.

As noted, the doctrine is liable to caricature. There is a difficulty with portraying the Father as a punishing judge who needs to be appeased. The difficulty consists in holding together the image of a loving Father who readily and eagerly forgives with one who almost in a calculated fashion exacts punishment. It is tempting to allow one of these perceptions to cancel out the other so that either divine love or divine justice stands as the ultimate word about God. Equally difficult is the idea that the forgiveness of God is somehow dependent upon an historical act, almost as if God wishes to forgive but is unable to do so fully until some kind of mechanism has been set up which makes it possible. So the cross is portrayed as an ingenious way in which God can forgive human beings, as he has wanted to do all along, without selling out on his just government of the world. However, the cross then becomes God's way out of his own dilemma rather than a resolution of the human condition.

It is a strength that the doctrine of penal substitution takes seriously the wrath of God. Evangelicals have steadfastly resisted the wider theological embarrassment with this notion in modernity. It is impossible to remove the wrath of God from the Bible without fundamentally reconstructing its content. Emil Brunner had it about right when he said that 'a theology which uses the language of Christianity can be tested by its attitude toward the biblical doctrine of the wrath of God, whether it means what the words of Scripture say'.[11] Scripture reveals a God who is passionate in his love and in his anger. Yet the wrath of God should not be conceived as an attribute of God in the same way as his love:

the wrath of God is subordinate to his love. It is, as Luther was at pains to point out, God's strange and alien work.[12] If God hides his face in wrath from his people it is but for a moment, whereas it is with everlasting love that he has compassion upon them.[13] The wrath of God is fleeting by comparison with his love and the two are not to be seen as equally balanced attributes. God *is* love and it would be entirely wrong to claim that he *is* wrath. But even here we risk misstating the case as though wrath and love are opposed to one another. This is the very misapprehension which leads some to want to dispense with the wrath of God altogether. The love of God is holy love and God manifests ultimate resistance to anything and everything which tends to destroy the creatures who are the objects of his love. This accounts for his opposition to sin and evil. Divine wrath is therefore a manifestation of divine love. It is because he is the passionately loving God that he is provoked to righteous anger and indignation. These are to be seen as the pain of the divine love, the wounded love of the Father whom we resist and spurn. Sin is more than an offence against an abstract law. It is the breaking of a personal relationship, a wounding of the Father. And if God gives us up to endure his wrath, his intention in this is that we might come to our senses.

It is natural to want to protect the holy wrath of God from being identified with human anger tainted by sin. Yet even human wrath is not entirely sinful. Biblically, wrath and judgement concern the preservation and restoration of a community in which relationships have been ruptured. Anger is a signal that there has been a failure in relationships. By punishing or demanding contrition of the perpetrator the community asserts that the injury and the person injured matter. In this sense the contradiction of love is not wrath but indifference. Indeed, without such anger it would be doubtful whether a community would be truly human, and forgiveness would be in danger of being trivialized.

It is hard to see how this process can function without an element of retribution. When people offend against the community they inevitably alienate themselves from the very people upon whom their continued well-being depends. There are consequences to their actions which disadvantage and bring pain upon them. Even the withdrawal of co-operation from those who behave destructively is a form of retribution. A Christian perspective on this process need not deny the retributive element but should see beyond it to the restoration of the offender, who is also in varying degrees a victim of dehumanizing processes which have contributed to the offence.

These insights enable us to return to examine the cross as a manifestation of divine love and wrath in a new light. If there is failure in the evangelical approach to the atonement it consists in its interpretation of atonement in excessively juridical or forensic terms. This language can by no means be neglected since in very clear ways the crucifixion of Jesus was a forensic process involving a trial, allegations of breaking the law, judges and a judicial execution. Furthermore, the metaphors of law, judgement and justification are primary categories for interpreting the theological significance of the event. Yet this language, like all 'theories' of atonement, is itself metaphorical and suffers from limitations. Commonly, evangelical attempts to state the meaning of atonement in these terms require the listener to take on board a mental construct which begins with the existence of laws which human beings have broken, thus incurring guilt. This guilt is believed to have been transferred to Christ as a substitute. Forgiveness may therefore be extended in a way which satisfies the just requirements of the law and does not undermine it. Yet this explanation sounds mechanical and abstract and to that extent unsatisfying.

A relational perspective

The primary reality to which the various metaphors of atonement refer is surely relational; the relationship with God has been ruptured and needs to be restored. It is helpful here to recapture the original context for the legal and forensic language of Scripture in describing the atonement.

Modern concepts of law and justice construe the law as an abstract power to which all are accountable and seek to render the legal process impersonal and impartial. Punishment consists in being fined or imprisoned. The Hebraic context out of which Pauline imagery grew was by contrast highly personal. To offend against the community was to forfeit that community's support and to be excluded from its network of relationships. 'Justification' was not therefore an abstract declaration of lack of guilt but the concrete, relational action of being re-included within the life-giving community. When our understanding of the wrath of God moves out of this relational context it becomes distorted. The wrath of God then becomes the calculated response of a God who maintains his distance from his creation, rather than his passionate resistance and hostility towards the sinful actions of creatures with whom he is involved.

In the relational categories we have used, the expression of wrath is not necessarily destructive. It is a necessary part of that process whereby a person is made aware that there is cause for alienation and displeasure so as to recognize the fault, take responsibility for it and pass beyond it to a place where the alienation has been overcome and a new state of affairs prevails. If we relate this to the cross of Christ it enables us to see that Christ is engaging on our behalf in a process whereby as a human being he experiences that divine wrath and pain against human sin. This wrath would destroy any sinful person who endured its full force, but Christ is able to endure it on our behalf and to go where we cannot go. He recognizes the depths of human fault and takes responsibility for it on our behalf in order to pass beyond it and renew with God that quality of covenant relationship which God has always purposed. It is not that the cross is necessary for God in order that he might overcome his wrath. Rather, it is necessary for the forging of covenant relationship with human beings in such a way as to acknowledge fully human sin so as to pass beyond it to reconciliation.

Forgiveness should not therefore be seen as something which is made possible for God by the cross, as though he requires an external means to resolve his dilemma. The cross is instead an expression in time of an eternal reality which takes place in God's heart. The historical atonement is the expression in time of an eternal willingness to make atonement, and also an event in time for both God and human beings in which that atonement becomes a completed reality through Christ. At the cross, God's eternal will to forgive outcrops into time and takes form as an historical event with a before and an after ('It is finished!').[14]

It is sometimes objected that the linking of forgiveness with the cross is unnecessary because God can 'just forgive', as do human beings. We have recognized some truth in this in saying that God does not need an external, mechanical event to become capable of forgiving. But it is superficial to say that God, or anyone, 'just forgives'. In human terms, forgiveness is the most difficult thing of all to do. All true forgiveness involves a journey which is itself painful and costly.[15] The cross is the revelation of that cost in God whereby in eternity his compassion for human beings overcomes the pain they bring to him and the wrath which they excite, and then constitutes in human time a point at which the readiness for forgiveness becomes reconciliation. It is not necessary to enable God to forgive, but it is necessary that human beings may renew relationship with God in a way that does not deny or overlook the depths of their sin but rather brings it to full awareness and overcomes it.

More on wrath and judgement

In what has been written there is an accurate perception about the meaning of atonement. But the cross remains a greater event than any attempt to understand it, and lacking from the account we have given is the biblical notion that the wrath of God is also a *fate* or an eschatological declaration of divine refusal from which we need to be delivered.[16] The idea of the wrath of God has therefore not yet been exhausted. God is not only the one who seeks to restore relationship with lost creatures but also the one who maintains faithfulness to his creation and to its moral integrity. In creation, God reveals himself as he who sets things in order, and what is true of creation is also true of redemption. Wrath must be understood therefore both as a personal quality of God and as the fate which awaits those who resist and reject God. We find truth here in the sustained attempt of certain exegetes, most notably C. H. Dodd[17] and A. T. Hanson,[18] to find in Paul's exposition of divine wrath a process of cause and effect whereby sin brings upon itself its own judgement through unlocking consequences which are tragically destructive of the sinner. In this sense the wrath of God is also that fact of existence whereby we reap what we sow, to our detriment.

Dodd and Hanson wished to conceive the wrath of God as an impersonal process of cause and effect and so to exculpate God from the demeaning charge, as they perceived it, of being a wrathful God who needed to be appeased or propitiated by Christ's sacrifice. Unlike them, we have argued that wrath is a personal quality and have found no embarrassment in it. The wrath of God must be rooted in the divine being. Even if it does operate as a process of cause and effect this process exists because of the will of God and corresponds to his hostility towards evil. But once this is granted we can certainly acknowledge that *the way in which* the wrath of God comes upon people is by a process of cause and effect which is written into the fabric of the universe. The divine judgement takes place when, instead of preserving us from the effects of our own actions, God gives us over to them. Despite the fact that in the Bible highly personal language is used of God in describing his response to sin, the way this actually and primarily works out is through a process whereby God hands us over to the consequences of our own actions. This receives particular emphasis in Paul's reiterated phrase in Romans where he states three times that on account of people's sin, 'God gave them up' (1.24, 26, 28). It can be seen in the history of Israel: God gave his disobedient people over to the nations to be overcome and judged by them.

This alters the way we think of God's punishment. It is not that God 'takes his wrath out on us' but rather that he gives us up to experience the actual consequences of what we have chosen for ourselves. Paul Fiddes distinguishes here between 'extrinsic' and 'intrinsic' punishment,[19] the former being that which is inflicted on us from outside on account of our misdeeds, and the latter being that which arises from our deeds themselves and is their outcome. When conceiving of the wrath of God, we may think of it as intrinsic punishment.

There are direct consequences here for our formulation of penal substitution. We have already argued that atonement is a reality which takes place in the heart of God in eternity and which outcrops into time and becomes an historical event at the cross. We are not to think then of Christ appeasing or placating God to make him favourable towards sinners. Nor are we to conceive of the cross as an event of 'extrinsic' punishment whereby the Father personally punishes the Son instead of us (although as we have indicated there is a real experience of divine wrath here in the forging of a renewed relationship). Rather, the Father gives the Son over to redeem and restore the human race by participating in human existence and human fate. The Son of God enters into and identifies himself fully with fallen humanity to such an extent that he is able to represent humankind before God. This involves standing with us under judgement. In doing so he bears that 'intrinsic' punishment whereby sin produces alienation from God, becoming vulnerable to our self-inflicted judgement. By bearing this, Christ acknowledges the justice of the Father's judgement and says Amen to it in such a way, on our behalf, that he renounces and puts an end to the old, sinful humanity and replaces it with a new, obedient humanity.[20] The human situation is thus transformed and the possibility of a renewal of covenant with God opened up for all.

In this way we may conceive of Christ's work being both substitutionary, in that it is done in our place and on our behalf, and penal, in that it involves the bearing of an 'intrinsic' punishment, but not as 'penal substitution', with its implication of the Father personally punishing the Son. So the God who brings forgiveness does so in a way that fully acknowledges the reality of sin, does not pass over it but judges it, yet judges it so as to open the way to transformation. He shows himself as the one who justifies, putting things in order and maintaining his faithfulness to the creation and the moral foundation on which it rests. Redemption is by no means the denial or abrogation of creation but that still-creative activity of God whereby he restores creation to its intention in order that it may move forward through the impulses of the Spirit towards its goal. Redemption is a further manifestation of the divine power to create, to take the chaos of human sin and fallenness and from it fashion his gracious and redemptive purpose.

Transformational justice

Atonement is a process whereby God puts right what is wrong, restoring justice to the world. The 'judgement of God' should be seen in this light. It is not enough in speaking of God as judge to refer to his power to proclaim condemnation, as a human judge might do after verdict has been pronounced. A judge is one who presides over and facilitates a process which enables the truth to emerge. To be sure, when the truth has emerged it may prove necessary to condemn that which can clearly be seen to be in the wrong. But the object of judgement is that truth might emerge and the right prevail. So God's judgements in history are directed to this end, to bring to light the consequences of human actions so that illusions may be stripped away, lies and pretence be seen for what they are, and the truth vindicated. God's purpose in history is to establish justice. But it goes beyond this. He establishes justice in such a way as to enable the possibility of transformation and renewal. The justice which is revealed in the cross is not punitive but transformational, accepting human culpability for sin in such a way that the acknowledgement of the evil of the past can become the basis for present and future good.[21]

The cross of Christ therefore is the place where the truth about ourselves is in clearest focus and we know ourselves to be worthy of condemnation. But these realities are there faced and addressed in order that they might be removed and we be transformed. Indeed, the judgement of God here is a mercy because it frees us from deception and liberates us to find the truth.

What kind of God?

Evangelical approaches to the atonement have been at fault when they have made the penal substitutionary framework the only grid through which the work of Christ is interpreted and when they have framed this one approach in a way which invites caricature. They have been strong in their insistence on the centrality of the cross, the objectivity of the work there accomplished, and the indispensability of the themes of wrath and judgement in our understanding of God. We have offered a series of reflections which enable us to preserve the strengths and avoid the pitfalls. There are areas with which we have not dealt and which would be essential to a full exposition. Not least of these is that reflection upon which we are bound to engage after the horrors of Auschwitz and Hiroshima concerning what the cross reveals of the divine capacity to suffer. In the cross, God in Christ so partakes of and takes up into himself the sufferings of his fallen creation that he is qualified to be the God of the outcast and the forsaken.[22] Yet the exposition we have offered should be seen in this light. Through the cross, God has qualified himself through his entry into human experience and his endurance of our fate to be the one who can come to our rescue and be, in the fullest sense of the term, our saviour. Vernon White expresses this as follows:

> God in Christ takes into his own divine experience that which qualifies him to reconcile, redeem, and sanctify in his relationship with all people everywhere . . . [I]t is something like the mountain guide who first crosses a difficult terrain himself, in order to take across all who will follow him. It is a journey we could not make apart from him, yet must make. It is, of course, the journey of dying to self and living wholly to God – through temptation, suffering, and death itself.[23]

We are thus in a theological world which is far removed from mechanical theories of atonement. God himself is our hope and, this said, we are able to take up the full range of biblical and theological metaphors to capture the range of what he has entered into and accomplished for us. The cross, therefore, becomes not an external instrument of salvation but the very revelation of God's own being and of his way of reconciling the world to himself. It is the very expression of the God whom we confess and the pattern of our response to him and imitation of him. It is indeed that which should test all our theology and our actions.

6

The Legacy of Liberalism

Contemporary evangelicalism must include liberalism among the forces which shape it. We are heirs to the liberal legacy. This will sound offensive to many evangelicals who regard themselves as the opponents of liberalism. It all comes down, of course, to what we mean by 'liberalism' and how we conceive of being its heirs. In this chapter, I argue that liberalism, like many other movements, has made both a positive and a negative contribution to the Church's life. While we do well to resist the negative, we are foolish not to embrace the positive. Furthermore, distance allows us freedom to draw upon the positive without fear of compromise.

The roots of liberalism

The origins of liberal Christianity go back to the eighteenth century and to the critical philosophy of the Enlightenment. This shift in Western ways of thinking called traditional authorities into question and replaced them with a new emphasis on the principle of doubt and upon the competence of reason to determine what was acceptable in the traditions. In the philosophical realm, metaphysical systems of belief began to collapse under the sceptical methodologies of Hume and Kant. In the scientific realm, the escalation of new discoveries encouraged the notion that human understanding of the world was evolving and improving. What belonged to the past was therefore more likely than not to prove mistaken in the light of new knowledge. The past might still be considered valuable, provided it were passed through the sieve of reason. Liberal Christianity is that form of response to these developments which, in order to present Christian faith in a way which was relevant and persuasive, accepted the forms of thinking which had developed and sought to reconstruct Christianity along those lines.

In practice, therefore, certain characteristics are foundational to liberal Christianity: a willingness to accept the methods and assumptions of historical enquiry; a preference for the inner and experiential aspects of religion over against dogmas and creeds; a generally positive appraisal of the progress of human civilization and ways of thinking, including the assumption that the new tends to be superior to the old; a concern for morality and social relevance; and characteristically Enlightenment concerns for individuality, human rights, toleration, political liberation and social emancipation.

Liberalism has come under severe censure for neglecting the more rugged and angular aspects of the Christian tradition, such as sin and guilt, and for its anthropological starting-point. Richard Niebuhr's famous criticism that it degenerates into sentimentalism, as 'a God without wrath brought men without sin into a Kingdom without a cross', is much to the point. Despite this we maintain that there are resources to be gathered as we pursue today's mission.

Light in the Enlightenment

It is impossible to list the qualities of liberalism, as we have done, without at some points wanting to affirm them. There certainly is 'light' in the 'Enlightenment' and in the religious variations it spawned. Indeed, some of this light we believe to be a product of the cumulative influence of Christianity within Western culture and of Free Church Christianity in particular, with its emphasis on the priesthood of all believers and the Christian congregation. Radical Christians had been experimenting for some time before the Enlightenment with new ways of being the Church, rejecting hierarchies, involving all members in congregational decisions, appointing their own leaders, insisting upon religious liberty and the rights of conscience and setting limits to what rulers might demand of their people. These theological innovations of the sixteenth and seventeenth centuries amongst Anabaptists and radical Puritans helped prepare the way for the political changes of the eighteenth century and beyond. The description of the Enlightenment as Christianity's 'rebellious child' is not inaccurate.

But we have now lived long enough and seen enough in a world shaped by the Enlightenment to be aware of the ambiguities of it all. The benefits of scientific discovery and the growth of technology are immense and no one would want to put the clock back; yet, more recently, scientists generally have come to be seen not as the new high priesthood of human progress but as the developers of new possibilities of global destruction, experiments on animals and environmental pollution. Undoubtedly we have grown in political understanding and modern democracies have eliminated many of the routine brutalities and inequities of previous systems; but we have also become increasingly socially fragmented and alienated from each other and have lost the sense of organic cohesion and harmony which is a feature of more traditional societies. Both social democracy and free-market capitalism take their rise from the Enlightenment. Both democracies, with their freedoms and open debate, and the now-defunct Marxist tyrannies, with their lack of them, belong to a trajectory which begins in the Enlightenment.

In short, there is light in the Enlightenment but it needs to be discriminated and this in turn implies that Enlightenment thought must be tested against other authorities not predetermined by the Enlightenment itself. For the Christian, that authority will be the vision of God which is made known in Jesus Christ and witnessed to by the Scriptures.

As with any other aspect of created reality, Enlightenment thought might be a useful servant but is a poor master. Its value depends upon whether we consider its postulates to be absolute or relative. Where it is taken to be the case that the criteria developed by the Enlightenment are truths which are beyond question, it cannot but prove to be in conflict with Christianity. To accept its postulates, for instance that science and reason hold the keys to all knowledge or that human beings are accountable to no one but themselves, as *absolutes* or self-evident axioms, and then accommodate Christianity to them, inevitably leads to the deconstruction of Christian faith into something else. At this point, Enlightenment thought becomes a rival system, and one which has no place for religions which play any other than supine and legitimating roles for its own ideology. Liberal Christianity, in so far as it assumes this role, is a form of apostasy. But in that it wishes to learn from the *relative* truths of the Enlightenment and be true to them, it plays a valuable role within Christian faith.

Here we may distinguish between the positive and the negative aspects of religious liberalism. If the word 'liberal' means openness to other points of view, if it implies respect for others and refusal to penalize or punish others for the views that they hold, it is surely an honourable term. But expressed like this, 'liberal' theologians are to be found in many places as adherents of a variety of schools of thought. Without hesitation we can say that in this sense evangelicals certainly ought to be liberals. But when 'liberal' implies that the postulates of the Enlightenment are themselves taken as dogmas, then in effect we are dealing with an alternative religion.

There is a self-deceiving quality to this position in that in the name of freedom, tolerance and liberality, a system is advanced which can be every bit as illiberal and intolerant as the theologies it claims to oppose. It excludes the possibility that any truth claims other than its own can actually be true. The modern tactic is to marginalize religious truth claims by labelling them as 'fundamentalist'. By contrast with this is the importance of *conviction*, of being persuaded about what we believe, but of holding these convictions with the kind of humility which does not make absolute our own position, renounces imposing it upon anyone, and respects the convictions of others. This we hold to require a higher quality of tolerance than that of dogmatic liberalism because it accepts the starkness of the differences between people.

All truth is God's truth

Whereas the more conservatively inclined might believe that all truth can be read out of the Bible or must be legitimated by it, that the Bible on its own is sufficient for the human intellect, the liberally inclined take a more dialectical view. God has given the Bible as a source of theological understanding, but he has given rational capacities and abilities that we might explore the world God has also given us. There are, in this sense, two books in which we may learn of God: the book of God and the book of nature. Both need to be read simultaneously, to be compared and contrasted. Ultimately, if all truth belongs to God and all things cohere in him, we might reasonably expect there to be no *final* contradiction between what we learn of God in Scripture and what we learn of his world from any other source. There are good grounds for believing that this in fact represents the classic evangelical position.

At this point it is entirely right to recognize the relative nature of our quest for understanding in all spheres. Not only should we recall how little we know, but we should also retain a high degree of self-criticism about how we interpret what we do know. The more conservative have been entirely right at this point to advocate avoiding premature acceptance of the 'assured results' of modern enquiry, whether historical or in the realm of scientific theory. With the perspective of hindsight it becomes clear that both historians and scientists have the inclination to reproduce their premises in their conclusions, whatever their claims to objectivity.

The provisionality which belongs to the wider intellectual endeavour does not mean there cannot be growth in understanding. In the same way, although the Christian believes there is assured revelation in the biblical witness, our *understanding* of it remains provisional. At many points there may appear to be points of conflict between the world as we observe it and theological truth as we have grasped it; this is not to say that they are necessarily in ultimate conflict but that understanding needs to increase on all sides. There is a constant need therefore for multi-disciplinary reflection on how biblical witness relates to other disciplines and this will involve a willingness to live with unresolved tensions alongside apparent solutions. In that liberalism challenges us to take this enterprise with great seriousness and to refuse to avoid it, its legacy is to be embraced.

The humanity of Scripture

Liberal Christianity, in taking up the tools of historical criticism gained from the Enlightenment, has enabled us to appreciate more completely the humanity of Scripture. In asserting both the divine inspiration and full humanity of Scripture, the tendency is to resolve the tension between these two affirmations by allowing the 'divinity' to eclipse the 'humanity'. We are so wanting to stress the value of the Bible as the vehicle for the Word of God that we risk denying its sheer humanity in being this vehicle.

The Enlightenment witnessed a new interest in historical enquiry. It was no longer considered adequate to accept the interpretations of history passed down by the received authorities of Church and ruling class. By returning to primary sources and discovering what actually has happened in the past, a critical tool was discovered for calling traditional beliefs into question. This can be seen as an extension of Protestant logic: Protestants had called tradition into question by reaching beyond it to the very source documents of the faith. These then provided the criteria by which traditions could be tested and possibly rejected. Within liberal Protestantism this process was extended to reach back even beyond biblical interpretations of Christ to the historical Jesus (reconstructed by liberals), who was then used to test and deny the christological claims of the New Testament and of orthodox Christianity themselves. On this count, the simple prophetic figure of Jesus could never have believed himself to be the incarnation of God, and any subsequent belief to this effect was rejected as elaboration.

The flaw in the liberal Protestant approach consisted in the clumsiness of its historical methodology. The 'history' they reconstructed, while they believed it to be 'factual', in fact fashioned Jesus in their own image. They had decided upon the outline of what they were looking for before starting the task. This 'liberal' Jesus was in time devastatingly exposed by Albert Schweitzer's survey of their attempts[1] and is summarized in Fr Tyrell's celebrated comment that the Jesus they discovered was merely 'the reflection of a Liberal Protestant face seen at the bottom of a deep well'. Caution is necessary in evaluating 'objective' reconstructions of history. Granted this, critical scholarship has opened up new perspectives upon the nature, authorship, formation and function of Scripture. The net result of this is to enhance the value of the Bible for us by opening up more precisely the ways in which, acting in grace, God imparts his Word. Critical scholarship is by no means the exclusive preserve of the liberally and sceptically inclined. The resurgence of more conservative scholarship is well under way. However, it cannot escape notice that conservative scholarship is not what it was but has gained immeasurably from the more 'liberal' scholars with whom it is in dialogue. In the process it has moved on to new levels of insight, for instance in appreciating the varieties of literature in the canon and the differing theological perspectives behind them.

The Bible is both like and unlike other forms of human literature. It is through the humanness of Scripture that God's Word addresses us. It is folly to wish to protect the Bible from those things of which God himself is not ashamed. A docetic attitude to Scripture which will not allow it to be *completely* human (which is different from being *only* human) is misconceived. The Bible is to be investigated in the same way and by the same criteria as other works of literature. But when this has been done and it has been pronounced fully human it is still the vehicle of God's Word. The continuing debate concerns what the implications of this are. As there are analogies here with the incarnation, and as the humanity of Christ is usually appealed to as the model for understanding the Bible, it is appropriate first to turn to Christology.

The human face of Christ

We return briefly to the quest for the historical Jesus, the essence of which we have already described. Despite its failings we can discern a deeply religious motivation which lent excitement to the quest. In the eighteenth century Jesus was being rediscovered. It felt as though the layers of metaphysical overlay with which Jesus had been burdened for centuries was being stripped away in order that the personality of Christ might be discovered afresh. The essence of Christianity was regarded as devotion to Christ and a humble following after him.

There is something very right about this instinct and it remains among the greatest aspects of the liberal legacy. More orthodox approaches (and liberalism questions orthodox theology not just evangelical faith) run the danger of losing the earthly Jesus in the heavenly Lord, or of regarding his life as merely the prelude to the saving work of the cross. Orthodox Christianity easily overlooks the historical Jesus and so downgrades the themes of discipleship and of imitation of Christ. Liberal Christianity helps to restore the balance. Christianity has found some difficulty in coming to terms with the complete humanity of Christ and has suffered from an incipient docetism, the attribution to Christ of an apparent humanity and not a real one, which has shied away from full-blooded recognition of the implications of its own theology. The Church's Nicene and Chalcedonian Creeds assert the full humanity and the full divinity of Christ. The Church's understanding of salvation follows the dictum of Gregory Nazianzen that 'the unassumed is the unhealed'. To heal and restore humanity it was necessary for Christ to assume the fullness of human experience, to reach down into the full extent of fallen human nature. Despite this there has been a reluctance to work through the implications. Common experience shows that docetism is alive and well and living not least among evangelicals. As an abstract concept, the assertion of full humanity is accepted. As an actuality, when the details are added to the basic assertion, it is shied away from. Docetism might be described as the 'most orthodox heresy' since it honours the divinity of Christ, but only at the cost of repressing his humanity.

With the Enlightenment, reflected in liberal Christianity, there took place a shift towards an anthropocentric way of thinking. Instead of beginning reflection upon the world with God and his revelation, the quest for truth began with what human beings could know and confirm for themselves. This anthropological concern led to a new perspective on Christ and his work. It was no longer so necessary to find a Christ who could reconcile to God; instead, a Christ who could humanize human beings was required. Christ was a Saviour in that he exemplified in his own life and then inspired in others the best kind of humanity, demonstrated supremely in the loving sacrifice of the cross. By imitating Christ we could learn to share his own awareness of God and so be assimilated into his kind of humanity. This account of Christ's saving work is, from an orthodox perspective, incomplete. But it is *untrue* only if it claims to give a full account. The orthodox exposition of Christ's saving work also needs to deal adequately with this dimension and is in fact well equipped to do so. But in doing so it will inevitably draw gratefully on pioneering work which the liberal tradition has begun.

What are the implications of claiming that Christ assumed full and complete humanity? Christ's was both *real* humanity and *true* humanity, and these are not quite the same thing. By saying that he was *truly* human we point to a distinction between Christ and ourselves. Sinful humanity such as we all share is not true humanity since it does not centre on or ground itself in God. There is a fundamental flaw to it, in that we are self-centred people, turned in upon ourselves. According to Reinhold Niebuhr,[2] human beings exist in the tension of being creatures bound to the earth and guided by instinct, as with other animals, and yet being simultaneously aware of a destiny which reaches beyond the physical creation and is not exhausted by it. This duality gives rise to an anxiety which is not itself sin but which becomes the occasion for sin. The anxiety is rightly resolved by trusting in God and finding identity and security in him; indeed, it exists in order to cause us to seek after God and find him. But instead we seek escape from the anxiety by one or both of two responses: we find security in ourselves by exalting ourselves into the place of God and building our security around ourselves, or we smother our insecurity by immersing ourselves in our lusts and passions. The first response gives rise to the will for power, establishing our own importance by first gaining and then preserving domination over others. By contrast with these false responses, Jesus entered into the anxiety and tensions of human existence yet lived as we do not, as the one who 'did not consider equality with God something to be grasped',[3] as a servant in humble obedience to God.

Christ lived among us as the true human being, as the 'last Adam'[4] or the 'ultimate man', the exemplar and fulfilment of humanity, who, through death and resurrection, offered to the Father on our behalf the sacrifice of an acceptable life. He accomplished what we are unable to achieve for ourselves. In this sense, then, Christ's humanity was full of grace and truth to the extent that he is distinguished from other human beings. Yet apart from sin he was like us in every respect, fully acquainted with the pressures and temptations of being human.[5] Christ differs from us in his true humanity but is one with us in the *real* humanity which he assumed. We need to raise questions about what this involved.

There has been much debate as to whether the humanity Christ assumed was 'fallen' humanity, such as our own, or whether in Mary's womb he took upon himself an untainted nature, not prone to the same inclinations as ourselves. Some have understood the virgin birth to be an indication of precisely this: the inherited stain of original sin was interrupted through the virgin birth and Christ assumed an 'Adamic' nature, the kind of humanity borne by Adam prior to the fall. In order to protect Jesus further from the taint of original guilt and sin, Mary's own humanity came to be regarded by the Catholic tradition as itself protected miraculously from original sin through the 'immaculate conception'. Certain Anabaptists developed a parallel doctrine of the 'heavenly flesh' of Christ. Apart from the lack of biblical warrant for these positions, they tend in the wrong direction in that they remove Christ from the humanity he came to redeem and lessen the sense that he came to where we are, assuming our kind of humanity in order to redeem it. The implication of this crucial pattern of thought is actually that Christ assumed fallen humanity.

This is not to say that Christ himself was sinful but that he entered into human experience as it had become as a consequence of the fall. By entering the continuum of human existence as in its fallenness it has come to be, he opened up the possibility of its being healed and renewed from within. The virginal conception is therefore a sign of God's initiative, of the new work in which he is engaged. As the Spirit brooded over the waters at the creation of the earth, so the same creative Spirit overshadowed Mary to bring about an act of new creation, the creation first in Christ and then through Christ of a new humanity. The value of the virginal conception is not its miraculous content as such, although this is fitting, but its role as a sign pointing to the conception and birth of Christ by the Spirit.

To think of the incarnation in these terms requires us to develop once more a trinitarian model of thought. When the Son of God assumed human nature he did so in reliance upon the Spirit of God, being born of the Spirit and empowered by the Spirit in the fulfilment of his mission. To recognize the role of the Spirit in the coming of Christ allows us greater freedom in acknowledging the full humanity of Christ. Christ did what he did because he lived in human dependence upon the Spirit who was the activating presence in all his works. He was indeed the Son of God become flesh for our salvation, but as one who was fully human he lived and worked as we are required to do, in dependence upon the Spirit. This brings Christ closer to us. It also establishes a line of continuity between his humanity and our own. The same Spirit who was at work in Christ is given through Christ to continue his work in us.

Christ and the capacity for 'error'

At this point we hit a crunch issue in spelling out the humanity of Christ: could Christ have been wrong? Here the assertion of the divinity and humanity of Christ comes into play: to affirm his divinity might lead us to stress his 'inerrant' status; to affirm his humanity surely involves the capacity, which we all share, to get things wrong. Does the assertion of the capacity for error require us to abandon the belief that Christ is the Truth who teaches the ways of God truly?

A careful distinction is necessary here, which is often missed in discussing both Christ and the Bible. The word 'error' has come to carry certain moral overtones, especially for Christians. To describe someone as being 'in error' implies that they are at best badly mistaken and at worst quite heretical. To describe either Christ or the Bible as being in error in this way would certainly be a devastating blow. Neither would be reliable guides. In short, to be in error and deceive people is a moral failing, whether deliberate or otherwise. Yet this is, I believe, to be clearly distinguished from an innocent mistake which, although unfortunate, is scarcely culpable.

In this sense mistakes belong to the very nature of being human. We are radically limited. Although some make more mistakes than others, to err is indeed human. In the process of typing this manuscript I am constantly making mistakes, largely because I am a self-taught typist and have developed all the bad habits a properly trained person knows how to avoid. The most used button on my word processor is the one which deletes! What is true in this one area is true in varying degrees of everything I do. This is not primarily to do with the undoubted fact that I am sinful (although were I not I would no doubt do everything in a more thoughtful and disciplined fashion, even learning to type). Innocent mistakes are, rather, an element in my humanity, a symptom of the fact that I am much less than God. When we learn any new skill we do so by being allowed to make mistakes along the way. Frankly, I would have it no other way. If human beings were inherently inerrant they would be insufferable. Our limitations drive us to dependence upon God and upon each other, and that need and capacity for interdependence and co-operation is one of life's greatest joys.

There should therefore be no difficulty in acknowledging that Jesus was capable of innocent mistakes; indeed, it becomes necessary to believe that he was so, otherwise we would once more be making his humanity apparent rather than real. The trinitarian model of incarnation enables us to conceive of Jesus' humanity more clearly. He is no combination of divinity and humanity with all the paradoxes that creates as to how the omnipresent can be spatially limited or the omniscient possessed of less than complete knowledge. Rather, he is the expression of the divine freedom which includes the capacity to achieve its purpose even through assuming human limitations and weakness; he is the manifestation of the divine wisdom which can pursue its purpose successfully even by surrendering itself for humanity's sake to the capacity for innocent mistakes. We might speculate here about the ways in which Jesus 'grew in wisdom and stature'[6] or upon the fact that 'although he was a son he learned obedience from what he suffered'.[7] As one who was fully and really human, Jesus learnt in the way that we all learn, at times by trial and 'error'. If Jesus had learnt mathematics it is inconceivable that he would automatically and immediately have known all the right answers. Being human involves submission to the ways humans learn, and this involves innocent mistakes, sometimes getting things wrong before we can get them right. As a carpenter, Jesus would not automatically have known how to do everything. He would have made a mess of things from time to time and, indeed, may not even, for all we know, have been a brilliant carpenter. There are no moral judgements involved in this, simply the recognition that skills are not equally apportioned. To insist that Jesus was a prodigy or a genius at everything he did removes him from those of us who can do some things tolerably well, other things poorly and most things not at all.

The pattern of thought developed here is actually confirmed by the gospel record. I am asserting that as the faithful and true witness[8] to his Father, Jesus speaks truly, accurately and with authority on those things central to his mission, but that this does not imply that he was incapable of innocent mistakes in other areas. Two specific occasions in the Gospels confirm this. In Mark 2.25–6 Jesus cites the incident when David ate the consecrated bread in the house of God 'in the days of Abiathar the high priest'. 1 Samuel 21.1–6 indicates that *in fact* Ahimelech was priest, only to be succeeded after his death at the hands of Saul by his son Abiathar (2 Sam. 8.17). Similarly Jesus refers in Matthew 23.35 to 'Zechariah son of Berakiah, whom you murdered between the temple and the altar', whereas 2 Chronicles 24.20–1 indicates that the Zechariah who was murdered was in fact the son of Jehoida. Zechariah son of Berakiah was the prophet responsible for the book that bears his name (Zech. 1.1). On the face of it, it looks as though Jesus has made here two simple and innocent mistakes of detail similar to those that most of us make every day of our lives.

True enough, it is possible to argue against these observations: to speculate for example that Ahimelech and Abiathar shared the high priesthood in the same way that Annas and Caiaphas were later to do,[9] or that Zechariah may have been the son of Jehoida but could have been the grandson of one named Berakiah, and that the Hebrew custom often employed the formula 'son of' simply to indicate descent. There is no evidence for these speculations, so they can neither be proved nor disproved and those who choose to believe them are entitled to do so. Alternatively, it could be claimed that Jesus was right but that either his words were wrongly recorded so that the biblical writers are in error or that the Old Testament text had it wrong and that Jesus was correcting it. Yet those who employ this argument are usually also committed to an inerrant biblical text and so this opens up for them a further problem. The most honest approach, unless we are determined by all means possible to maintain an *a priori* assumption that Jesus could never have been wrong about anything, is to accept the most obvious interpretation and agree that Jesus, apparently, was capable of innocent mistakes.

If Jesus was really human, and if human beings are inherently limited and capable of such mistakes, why should this disturb or even surprise us? Jesus did not have our access to a copy of the Bible which he could constantly refer to. He would hear the Scriptures read in the synagogue and sometimes would read them there himself. The human memory can be a superbly accurate instrument but is also always limited. The text simply confirms about the humanity of Jesus what we profess to believe about him anyway, namely the completeness of his humanity. This is a cause for wonder rather than for worry since it indicates that Jesus really was one of us and one with us. The capacity for innocent mistakes in no way qualifies his authority in bearing witness to those things that were integral to his mission. The sooner we drop our stained-glass window approach to Jesus the better. Liberalism recognized this a long time ago.

The Bible and the capacity for error

The incarnation is often taken as the illustration of the way in which by analogy the Bible can be both divinely inspired and fully human. Christ was fully human and yet without error, we are told. Similarly, the Bible is divinely inspired and fully human, and its humanity does not of necessity mean that it must at points be in error. Apart from the fact that there is not an exact analogy here (Christ was more than a divinely inspired human and God is not incarnate in the Bible), the distinction we have made between morally blameworthy errors and innocent mistakes qualifies the sense in which Christ was 'without error'. Christ does not lead us astray but was capable of innocent mistakes. Likewise, the Bible does not leads us astray. When correctly used and understood it establishes itself as the reliable witness to the God who acts and speaks in Christ. But the biblical writers are capable of innocent mistakes. This does not compromise their central witness or the Bible's authority any more than mine would be invalidated if I am witness to a crime and in giving my testimony in court I am less than totally accurate in some minor detail. This is to be expected and might even increase the value of the testimony.

The liberal spirit

We have set out in this chapter various ways in which liberal Christianity bequeaths its legacy to following generations. In subsequent chapters further areas of this legacy will be taken up, although as part of a dialogue wider than that with liberalism itself. These areas include the social gospel, optimism with regard to human salvation and the openness of spirit that the liberal tendency has exemplified at its best. It is foolish to refashion Jesus as a first-century version of a modern liberal; it is equally foolish to deny that liberalism captured something of Christ's humanity expressed in his compassion and mercy. To be sure, some evangelical traditions have never lost sight of this, particularly those in the Anabaptist stream which emerged in sixteenth-century Europe, for whom the humanity of Jesus has been a constant inspiration and has enabled them to keep alive, in ways others neglected, the theme of discipleship, of conformity to Christ. Notable here is their commitment to the non-violent way of Jesus. When these themes become detached from the wider story of the grace of the Father and the presence of the Spirit they can degenerate into sterile imitation. Yet set within a full trinitarian narrative, the humanity of Christ can shine forth in its self-giving, servant-like love as the normative expression of what God wills for all and makes possible for all through the work of the Son and by the power of the Spirit.

7

A Kinder, Gentler Damnation?

In chapter 2 I argued that one strength of evangelical faith was its capacity to hold on to unpopular ideas. Its commitment to a robust statement of the wrath and severity of God, rooted in love, is an example of this. I also signalled the need to return to the question of the 'larger hope', the belief that the scope of salvation reaches further than current evidence suggests. The doctrine of election and divine freedom expounded in chapter 2 provides us with a basis of hope for the whole world of humanity, rooted in the objective and universally significant work of Christ. This chapter enquires further concerning the actual outworking of what is rendered potential by Christ's work. Will those who are saved be many or few?[1]

Evangelicals do not support the dogmatically universalist stance that all will attain to final salvation. Chapter 2 set out a non-dogmatic, hopeful universalism which refused to limit either the love or the freedom of God. This both changes our perspective in considering the lost, making us hopeful, and does not fall prey to bland and sentimental optimism, keeping us realistic. Evangelicals have also held firmly to a doctrine of hell and a high view of human responsibility. Moral decisions made in this life have eternal consequences for good or ill. Hell has been conceived as eternal, conscious torment. The difficulty of such a doctrine has also been felt, and evangelical voices offering alternative understandings have not been lacking.[2] This chapter deals with these questions in the belief that they are determinative for evangelicals.

The primacy of personal salvation

The evangelical habit of thought places great stress on the matter of personal, eternal salvation. This is the underlying question that accompanies popular evangelical thinking and instincts: 'Is this person saved?' or 'Will they go to heaven?' is a first concern. It would seem to me healthier to be more focused upon God's purpose for his creation as a whole, and to be asking the alternative question, 'How will God be glorified?' The passion for 'souls', for the eternal salvation of persons, is in itself commendable and accounts for evangelicalism's relative strength while other forms of Christianity, less determined to win converts, are in decline. If you really do believe in hell you will certainly want to rescue people from it. The concern, however, is whether making the matter of personal salvation the *primary* or *defining* issue is itself helpful or whether it causes the neglect of other necessary matters. Yet it does seem clear that the evangelical pattern of thought is so deeply ingrained, and raises such important questions, that it must be addressed before it is possible to move on to new ways of thinking in other areas.

Hell as eternal torment

It is not the general concept of 'hell' but its content that is here contested. There are forms of self-imposed or humanly created hell, the way our sins isolate us from other people, for instance. The Bible refers to more than this, however, and does so in a way that cannot be brushed aside. Hell is interpreted by evangelicals to be the ultimate destiny of the impenitent, a state of eternal, conscious torment. Nothing less is adequate retribution for human sin. To downplay hell is seen as reducing the gravity of sin and the offence it causes to God.

Plainly there are difficulties here. We are asked to believe that a finite quantity of sin committed in time is rightly recompensed by an infinite quantity of torment in eternity. This seems to fly in the face of the principle of proportionality.[3] By what scale of justice does finite sin, however horrendous, deserve infinite recompense? The standard response to this employs a feudal argument based on the person of the overlord: it is the infinite worth of the divine person offended that constitutes the infinite culpability of the sin. Human sinners are thus rendered liable to judgement of eternal duration because of the one against whom they have sinned. When the further objection is raised that this denies all human understandings of justice, we are told that God's justice is other than fallen human justice and what to us appears unjust may in fact in God's eyes be just.

As cast, however, this discussion leans in the wrong direction. The ultimate reality about God is not the iron logic of his justice and his laws but the illogical extravagance of his love. God's essence is not wrath but love. Wrath is a temporary manifestation of his holy love, but not the last word. Some, of course, insist that human ideas of divine love are hopelessly sentimental. The holy God is true love and is free to save or damn human beings without compromise to his loving nature. Others object that this places divine love in a category which is gratuitous rather than gracious. Yet a doctrine of hell might be grounded in the love of God[4] by insisting, in my view quite rightly, that love does not ultimately override the will of the one who is loved. It can draw, persuade and seek to win another, but it cannot coerce the response of love. If human beings harden themselves against divine love they may well come to the point of no return, to a state of self-willed inability to do other than resist God's love. If a person is intent on suicide it is a human responsibility to persuade them otherwise. But when a person in full knowledge of the options has taken a calculated decision to forsake life, how could even the most loving person prevent the inevitable from taking place?[5] So with hell: the creation of free persons by the personal and loving God who seeks and enables free response cannot exclude the possibility of final loss.

Conditional immortality

Final loss of the impenitent is not, therefore, incompatible with the love of God; rather, its possibility is a deduction from it. This still offers us no help in assessing the claim that hell consists in everlasting torment. Eternal loss and eternal torture are hardly the same thing. The former might be defensible, but what about the latter? If it is believed that the human soul is inherently immortal, that it never ceases to exist but must endure eternally either in heaven or in hell, a concept of eternal torment might be inevitable. In this sense hell could be a state of metaphorical burning, being consumed by remorse, regret and the accusations of conscience after having received the vision of God which makes it absolutely clear what eternal love and beauty have been forfeited.

Yet it is hard to conceive of the redeemed enjoying eternal blessedness while being conscious of other human creatures in torment, many of whom will have been related to them in life. To argue that final judgement dissolves earthly bonds of connection, so that the anguish of the lost is no longer felt by the redeemed, is a convenient argument but a somewhat callous and not particularly convincing one. And how could we live in a new heaven and a new earth in which God is all in all[6] if in some part or dimension of that new creation there are creatures in torment?

The question in this argument concerns what is meant by the 'immortality of the soul'. This doctrine is well represented in the Christian tradition but many would agree that it owes more to Hellenistic philosophy than to the Hebrew background of Christianity. Often the term seems to denote the belief that the soul is able to outlive the body and that physical death is not the same as personal extinction. That the essence of human beings is not destroyed by physical death is certainly taught in the New Testament.[7] But this scarcely constitutes 'immortality' in the stronger sense of being 'incapable of dying'. In fact, Jesus spoke about the one who is able to destroy both body and soul in hell.[8]

All would agree that in the absolute sense only God has immortality.[9] Whatever 'immortality' is given to human beings is therefore derivative and relative. Since the New Testament clearly considers the enduing of *mortals* with immortality as an eschatological reality at the coming of Christ,[10] this suggests that they do not possess immortality even in a relative sense until and unless they attain that condition; consequently, both physically and spiritually they are capable of extinction, even if spiritual extinction does not coincide with physical death. This view is sometimes known as 'conditional immortality', since immortality is made dependent upon a new divine act of transformation.

This discussion heightens the difficulty of the doctrine of hell. If human beings are not inherently immortal then the only way they can suffer eternal torment is if they are eternally sustained in being by God. God therefore deliberately maintains potentially millions or even billions of human creatures in being in order to be tormented and does so because in their limited space and time they have offended against his person. It is extremely difficult to square this with the God of compassion and justice whom we encounter in and through Jesus Christ. The two visions of God bear no resemblance to one another. It helps not at all to argue that God's standards of justice are different from our own, since the obvious riposte is that such a God is inferior to human beings. If human beings would not do to their worst enemies what God, according to some, purposes to do to creatures whom he loves, then this kind of God is not worth believing in and it is hard to blame people who find it impossible so to do.

In fact the argument is unconvincing that God's justice is so far removed from human justice. Certainly, human perceptions of justice are distorted. Comparative studies show how they differ from social context to social context. But the root question here concerns whether there is a true revelation of God in Christ. If the only God who exists is the Christlike God who loves his enemies, the Father of Jesus Christ, it becomes impossible to believe in an inscrutable, hidden God who is other than what we see in Christ. Jesus did not deny the human sense of love and justice and its potential as an analogy for imaging God. He argued that God was so much more loving and more just than that. So: 'If you, then, though you are evil, know how to give good gifts to your children, *how much more* will your Father in heaven give good gifts to those who ask him!'[11] God's standards of justice and fairness are not less than the human, but so much more.

Exegetical evidence

The argument so far has not dispensed with hell, merely taken issue with one commonly held perception of it as eternal torment. While we see clearly in the Bible an expectation of future judgement and warnings of eternal loss, it is surprising how little direct support there is for the addition to this doctrine of the component of eternal, conscious torment. Those who wield the cudgels for and against this theme debate the indirect exegetical evidence from many points of view,[12] most of which discussions end up, in my judgement, being inconclusive. The direct evidence is contained in four contested passages, on which we shall focus.

Two of these passages are cast in clearly apocalyptic imagery. Revelation 14.9–11 describes those 'who worship the beast and its image' (that is, who comply with Rome and all such systems in their totalitarian idolatry) being tormented with fire and sulphur:

'the smoke of their torment rises for ever and ever' and 'there is no rest day or night'. Likewise in Revelation 20.7–15 the devil is 'thrown into the lake of burning sulphur where the beast and the false prophet have been thrown. They will be tormented day and night for ever and ever' (v. 10). Then death and Hades are thrown into the lake of fire to be accompanied by anyone whose name was not written in the book of life (vv. 14–15).

Interpretation of these verses must take account of the apocalyptic imagery in which they are couched. The Book of Revelation generally requires this appreciation of symbol and to insist on taking its words literally at this point would be inconsistent with the way the book is understood at most other points. The hyperbolic and metaphorical nature of the language is revealed in these passages when they refer to the beast (dictatorial Rome and regimes like it) and the false prophet (the religious emperor cult and other such false religions) being tormented day and night in the lake of burning sulphur. They are joined there by death and Hades. This is plainly the language of apocalyptic symbol and refers in powerful and memorable language to the way God will finally overcome all those powers opposed to him and establish justice once and for all. It is wise then to regard this language as 'non-inferential',[13] that is, not to infer from its pictorial imagery ideas which extend beyond its primary purpose of bearing witness in a figurative form to God's power to resolve fallen human history. This is to use it for a purpose not intended.

The other two verses occur on the lips of Jesus himself and so are to be treated with the greatest respect. In Mark 9.48, having previously warned his hearers three times of the danger of being thrown into hell, he cites Isaiah 66.24 to the effect that in hell 'their worm does not die and the fire is not quenched'. As in Isaiah, this is a reference to the terrible reality of divine judgement. To the south west of Jerusalem, and beyond its walls, the valley of Hinnom served as the rubbish dump for the city. It was filled with the smell of roasting flesh and contained the burning and rotting dead bodies of unwanted children, convicts and suicides which the citizens could go out and see at any time.[14] Ge-Hinnom, the Hinnom valley, thus became in New Testament Greek 'Gehenna', the word used to translate here Jesus' references to hell.

Jesus refers to the fact that there is an eternal place of judgement and disintegration corresponding and like to the Hinnom valley. But there is no necessary implication here of conscious eternal torment for those who doom themselves to hell. Hell itself may endure as a place or state of destruction; as in Ge-Hinnom there might continually be worms and fire to feed upon the dead. But the dead themselves have disintegrated. This is the force of the analogy. Once more, the reference to the horror of eternal judgement is expressed in metaphorical terms because all other language to describe the indescribable is lacking.

In Matthew 25.46, at the conclusion of the parable of the separation of the sheep and the goats, Jesus says: 'Then they [the goats] will go away to eternal punishment, but the righteous to eternal life.' Does 'eternal punishment' here imply conscious eternal suffering? The real significance here belongs to the word 'eternal' which is primarily a qualitative rather than a quantitative adjective: the life and punishment to be accorded at the last judgement have an eschatological character. This is not temporal life or punishment, which is meted out and which could be reversed, but that which belongs to the coming age, signifying inclusion in or exclusion from God's eternal Kingdom, final gain and final loss. Both grow organically out of the responses to God that have been given and lived out in this life.

There can be no doubt, then, that Jesus taught a doctrine of hell, unless we are prepared to argue that all such references[15] are later additions and are not original to Jesus. There was a sobriety to Jesus' teaching, but it is mistaken to claim him as an exponent of eternal torment.

Reconstructing hell

Hell is that reality created by the very being of the holy God when in the future he fills all things and makes himself directly present in every part of his creation. Tradition speaks of the 'four last things', heaven and hell, death and judgement. But when it comes down to it, there is only one last thing and that is God himself, the Alpha and the Omega,[16] the first and the last.[17]

The present age is one in which God has created space for human beings, for their lives to run their course. We are called to seek God and to find him, but might also resist and reject him. In the end we meet with God and there is no escaping him. It is this final encounter which spells heaven or hell. For the finally impenitent sinner who has resisted all the works of God to draw him or her out of themselves and to himself, this encounter means destruction, as it nearly did for Isaiah who on seeing the holy God cried out 'Woe is me! For I am *disintegrated*' (the literal meaning of the Hebrew).[18] It is inevitable that this be so, for this is the only way the person who rejects God can experience God.

Hell is not a place of eternal conscious torment in fire but an ultimate, final encounter with God. The lost do not simply cease to exist when they die physically; they are not quietly liquidated after the judgement when they have been restored to conscious and personal existence. The torment of hell consists in beholding God at the last, looking upon his beauty, majesty and infinite love and knowing that through one's own deliberate fault all of this has been made forfeit and lost. In short, hell is the *infinite loss of God*. Here is the moment of truth in the feudal idea that our sin against God's infinite person constitutes our infinite sin, yet it is now reversed. Our loss is as great as is God himself, since his eternal purpose has been to be our God and to become all in all to us.

Yet this infinite loss is forced upon no one. It is self-selected. As C. S. Lewis put it: 'There are only two kinds of people in the end: those who say to God, "Thy will be done", and those to whom God says, in the end, "Thy will be done".'[19] This by no means lessens the horror of hell. Rather, it clarifies in what this horror consists: not in fire, sulphur and burning, even throughout eternity, but in refusing and therefore losing the God who has love for us as his very being. Once more, our theology is personally and relationally defined not as torment in some eternal concentration camp, but as a falling out of the hands of the one who loves us. The horrific images of fire or darkness[20] capture something of the tragedy and pain, but ultimately the loss of God who is the source and ground of all life provides no way in which any creature could continue to be.

Enough has been said to show that this is no soft option, no kinder, gentler damnation, but a destiny to avoid, for God's sake and for our own.

The larger hope

It is good for evangelicals to remind themselves that no one goes to hell accidentally. I have argued that people are finally excluded from God's eternal and loving purpose only because they first of all exclude themselves. But here we must return to the themes we referred to in chapter 3.

The number of people who attain in this life to living relationship with God through conscious confession of Christ is much less than the total number of human beings. John Hick is right to remind us that 98 per cent or 99 per cent of people live and die in the religion into which they are born.[21] If a person's eternal destiny is tied up with how they have responded to Christ, how are we to account for the fact that the majority of them have never even heard, let alone heard sufficiently, the gospel which brings salvation? It is entirely true to claim that through general revelation and the witness that God maintains to himself throughout all generations[22] all people have some kind of access to the knowledge of God. In so far as they fail to respond to it they render themselves guilty. But this legalistic approach which weighs up quantities of guilt fails to reckon with what is at the heart of the Christian faith, namely the *illogicality* of the love and grace of God. The point is that God does not deal with human beings according to what they deserve but according to grace. He is the God who wills to save not to destroy.

There is a tension at this point within the Christian faith between the belief that God is a saving God who does not want anyone to perish[23] and the belief that there is only one mediator between God and humankind, namely Christ.[24] This universalist –particularist tension lies close to the heart of the faith, and to understand it correctly is of great theological importance. The 'scandal of particularity' (as it is called), the belief that God is uniquely and finally active in the specifics of the life of Jesus in a way which has universal significance, has been such an essential part of Christianity from the beginning that to deny it is in fact to depart from historic Christianity. But believing in it becomes increasingly more difficult the more we know of the world. The world is getting bigger. We now know, in a way that the Reformers or the apostles could not, just how much of the world there is that lies, apparently, outside the rule of Christ.

For the Reformers, Europe was Christian, the greatest majority of its population having been baptized in infancy and owing allegiance to either the Catholic or Protestant Churches. The discussion on hell carried the assumption that the majority were probably not destined for it anyway. For the apostles, the known world was the Mediterranean and Middle East and although this was large enough and minimally Christian it was at least possible intellectually to think about it in relation to Christ and believe in his significance for it.

Modern knowledge has expanded our concept of the world on several fronts. Geographically we are aware of its size and of the fact that the human population is both more diverse and more considerable than was previously imagined. Until the modern day missionary movement broke out of the European enclave, the Christian faith penetrated mainly the northern hemisphere. For most of history most people have not lived in earshot of the gospel. Moreover, human beings have lived on the earth for much longer than was formerly known. Our grasp of the number of people at a distance from the very particular Christian gospel has increased at a staggering rate. Huge numbers have died in infancy and childhood. Others have lacked the mental competence, for whatever reason, to take up the cross and follow Christ, even presuming they may have heard of him. Cosmologically, we have begun to grasp the sheer size of the universe so that the task of reconciling to Christ 'all things, whether things on earth or things in heaven'[25] surpasses our powers of imagination. An expanding universe renders the particularity of the Christian faith, its Christ-centredness, all the more difficult to sustain.

We are entitled to hope in the name of Christ that salvation is universally accessible, not limited by time or space or circumstance. The saving God renders possible the final salvation of all. His capacity to save is present with him wherever he is. He has qualified himself to be the Saviour of humanity and accomplished what is necessary for this purpose through the particular career of Jesus of Nazareth. As the risen Lord, Christ's saving power is not bounded by earthly human limitations. This is the larger hope: God in Christ has ways of reaching people which the Church does not have and does not know.

Christ – known and unknown

A crucial distinction here concerns the efficacy of Christ's work in its *ontological* and *epistemological* dimensions. Does a person need to know of Christ and to name him in order to enter into his renewing work? It can be inferred from some biblical texts that this may be the case and that the message of Christ has to be heard before it can be believed and his benefits secured.[26] Certainly through the gospel of Christ salvation is imparted to people. It ought to be preached, widely and well. The incontestable fact, however, that the saints of the Old Testament were in living relationship with God, that this must, from a Christian perspective, have been through Christ as the one mediator, and yet that they knew of Jesus of Nazareth only in hazy anticipation and certainly not by name, counts against the view that it is necessary to know of Christ by name in order to enjoy redemption. *Ontologically* they benefitted from Christ's saving work. *Epistemologically*, they did not know that this came through Christ, even though they received it as the gift of God.

If the Old Testament saints knew God in this way, it is open to us to believe that others may also. The God who is free over space and time can in grace impart himself wherever he is present and chooses so to do. God is revealed in Christ as the one who comes to seek and to save. He is not like this only at the point of the incarnation but in his universal presence to human beings. This is altogether different from the pluralist stance which argues for the parity of all religious traditions and believes that God, or 'Reality', is mediated through a variety of religious forms and mediators. Rather, it is to say that the God who uniquely defines himself in the life and death of Jesus Christ also acts beyond the boundaries of the covenant people not *through* the world religions as such but *despite* them. They do not constitute an insuperable barrier to the electing grace of God, although inevitably the religious inheritance of any believer will colour the ways in which God is imaged.

God has taken up into himself, through the incarnation, atoning death and resurrection of Christ, that which is needed by all human beings to secure their eternal redemption.[27] Christ has made the journey that we all need to make, dying to sin and rising in God. It was necessary for this work to be accomplished in human history since otherwise it remains unearthed and unrealized as a human reality. Christ's work is therefore more than a revelation of God's love. It is a bridge-building, reconciling work, an effective and once-for-all reality which holds good for all human beings. Taking up into himself the work that he has accomplished, Christ lives in and to the Father as the one in whom God's work is prolonged and extended as an effective reality. Yet, to participate in this work, the response of faith has to be awakened and given. Although this happens through the Church as it bears witness to the gospel, this is the primary earthly vehicle at God's disposal, not the only one.

The scope of salvation

The argument so far has affirmed the freedom of the saving God to call those whom he wills to himself. This still leaves us with unresolved questions concerning those who die in infancy or childhood (a large proportion in total of the human race), of those who through miscarriage or abortion never reach the point of birth, or who are deprived through handicap of certain basic faculties. Clearly there are questions here, which we do not intend to address, about the points at which personhood is formed and the capacity for personal response is present. Even if we could answer these, it is clear that they would not remove the questions we are exploring.

A controlling belief at this point, which is very firmly held but which I am questioning, is that death seals a person's destiny and that the condition in which a person dies is that in which they will for ever remain after death. This could be deduced from Jesus' parable of the rich man and Lazarus. Yet what was true of the rich man, that he had had many opportunities in listening to Moses and the prophets to respond to the word of the Lord and repent but had ignored them, is scarcely true of all or even of many. What was true for him and justly so, that death sealed his fate, may not therefore be true for others whose case is different.[28] Likewise, the 'proof-text' that humans are 'destined to die once and after that to face judgement'[29] does not necessarily mean what is often inferred. The emphasis here is on the once-for-all nature of the death of Christ, like the common human experience of death. It is true that after death we face judgement, but the passage specifies no time-scale. Nor does judgement necessarily mean the final pronouncement of condemnation or acquittal, but rather the clarifying and purifying work of God whereby the truth emerges, and this could in the final analysis go either way.[30]

It is usual to take refuge from the questions we are asking either by pleading agnosticism or by appealing to the mystery of election. In the latter case the argument can take several forms. It may be believed that amongst, for instance, children who die or those who have never heard the gospel God has his secret elect. Their death is therefore irrelevant since either they have been determined for salvation or not and death does not alter this situation. Yet the appeal to election in this way is incomplete unless it is believed that the grace of God overrules or abolishes human response rather than awakening it. If election is that gracious work whereby God draws us into free and personal response, there must be some space or opportunity to make this response. This requires us to posit some such realm beyond death for the elect who have died prematurely to respond to the Spirit's gracious initiative. I shall later return to this possibility in another form.

The appeal to agnosticism on the basis that the judge of all the earth will do right[31] is comprehensible but could be premature in the light of the clear assertion of God's will that none should perish. What we know of God in Christ and the Scriptures allows us to be more adventurous. We cannot claim that there are clear biblical assertions about the fate of those who have never heard, but we can engage in legitimate if tentative theological development.

There is the possibility of what is termed 'post-mortem evangelism'.[32] Either at the point of death or in some condition beyond death, all who have been deprived of the opportunity for faith in Christ in life are given that opportunity by direct encounter with Christ. This is not so much a 'second chance' as a first opportunity. Yet even this language betrays a perspective of which we are not in favour since we are not dealing with questions of 'chances' or barely minimal ways of satisfying 'fair play'. The grace of God is such that it extends to human beings that which is the opposite to what they deserve. Salvation is rooted in God's will to save, not in the reckoning of accounts. Legal metaphors of guilt and judgement certainly play their role in the Scriptures but the reality beyond the metaphor is relational and personal, it relates to God's search for fallen human beings and their response or otherwise to his initiative.

The key question, therefore, is not so much whether human beings can be redeemed beyond death as whether God's search for his fallen creatures is thwarted by death or continues beyond it. The judge of all the earth will certainly do right, but from the perspective we currently occupy it is reasonable to suppose that this includes a universal search to win human beings to relationship with himself which does not cease at the point of human death. By this point some people might well have excluded themselves from the divine life, but we cannot assume that in every case. Neither should we assume that 'post-mortem' evangelism must necessarily lead to universal salvation, as though people find it easier to believe once confronted beyond death with the living God. For all we know, it may be harder, the issues being more starkly presented. There is the enduring mystery of the human capacity to resist God to be placed alongside God's persistence in pursuing human beings. Somewhere between these two mysteries is the ultimate scope of salvation.

Whereas belief in a universal salvation may be neither tenable nor desirable, we are entitled to hope and believe that its scope will be much greater than we currently see, and it will cause us to marvel both at the justice and the infinite grace of the Christlike God.

The missionary mandate

Having developed this line of thought, it is inevitable that evangelicals will wish to know what its implications are for evangelism. If, although Christ remains the one mediator, preaching the gospel is not ultimately the sole way of becoming related to him, does this not undermine the motivation for missionary work?

This may indeed be the case if our motive for that mission is to rescue people from hell in the belief that unless they hear the gospel they are 'doomed to a Christless eternity'. But no one goes to hell accidentally. The motives for mission are greater and richer than this. We engage in mission because the Christian gospel is true, it enables human beings to find liberation and fulfil their destiny, because through it people receive the Spirit of the messianic age and come themselves to participate in his mission of redemption, and because through the gospel people learn how to give glory to God, Father, Son and Spirit. This seems to be enough motivation to be going on with.

We preach the gospel because it is true and to believe and do the truth is good for people and for the world; otherwise we are the prisoners of illusions. It remains the primary earthly means by which God's saving grace wins people to the response of faith. People are lost in that they are deprived of relationship with God and so estranged from their own true destiny. The gospel conveys the truth to them so that they might enter into life. In some cases it may well be that the gospel interprets a reality into which they have already entered. Christ is the name which therefore clarifies, purifies and undergirds the knowledge of God they already possess. This lends excitement to making Christ known because there are surprises in store concerning the ways he has gone before us. There is more to be said here, however.

There is a distinction between the saints of the old and of the new covenants. Although those of the old were true believers and had been made regenerate by the Spirit they were not living in the age of messianic fulfilment. It is for this reason that Jesus could say that 'he who is least in the Kingdom of God' is greater than John the Baptist, even though no one born of woman was greater than he.[33] This is not a way of putting John down, but of pointing to the turn of the ages that took place between John and Jesus and which John predicted.[34]

Jesus was the Messiah upon whom the Spirit was poured that he might be the agent of the messianic Kingdom and the mediator of the Spirit to the messianic community. If there are redeemed people, believers, beyond the Church this is not to say that they are yet 'Christians' or that there is no distinction between them and those who are in the Church. Those who have been incorporated into the body of Christ have become participators in the Holy Spirit in a way which was not true of Old Testament saints, but was only anticipated by them as a future, eschatological event,[35] nor is it yet true of those beyond the covenant people who may truly know God. The messianic age has to do with God's purpose in history and the gospel of Christ is preached in order that those whom God is calling might become incorporated into God's messianic people.

Cornelius and his household are examples of God-fearing people who believed in the God of Israel. As Gentiles they were outside the covenant people, yet they received the Spirit on hearing of Christ from the lips of Peter and became themselves members of the Church, to its great enrichment. Here are words of particular significance which assert that God does not show favouritism but accepts those 'from every nation who fear him and do what is right'.[36] Cornelius already knew God. Through Peter's preaching and the reception of the gift of the Spirit he was also incorporated into the messianic body of Christ.

This we believe to be crucial for understanding evangelism: it is the means whereby God through his Son and by the Spirit draws others into his missionary outreach. The motive which undergirds this is not the fear that without it people will go to hell, although there is certainly compassion upon those who are in a lost condition, but the love and generosity which are instilled into our hearts by the missionary Spirit of God and which seek to reclaim what has been lost. The ultimate motivation is to bring glory to

God, to serve that work whereby his splendour, beauty and goodness are made known and the world and its inhabitants are restored to their true equilibrium and creative fruitfulness now and in the age to come.

8

Radical Politics

The previous chapter was devoted to the question of the ultimate destiny of human beings. For many evangelicals this is synonymous with the question of salvation: salvation is the assurance of eternal life. In the last chapter, I made responses to this concern which expand the traditional evangelical horizons and give grounds for a wider hope. Having faced this question, acknowledged its importance and removed some of the anxiety surrounding it, the ground is now set for a wider discussion of the nature of salvation.

Evangelicals and social concern

An overly individualized version of salvation fails to plumb the depths of the biblical vision for God's world. There is now a general consensus to this effect amongst most thoughtful evangelicals. The reserving of 'salvation' to inner and future realities, so that it happens to the soul at and beyond death, can be seen in retrospect to reflect two major shifts in the social context of Christianity which have influenced the development of its theology.

The *Constantinian shift* took place in the fourth century when the Christians ceased to be a persecuted minority and were first tolerated, after the apparent conversion of Emperor Constantine and the Edict of Milan in 313, then favoured by him and his successors and finally elevated by Emperor Theodosius in 392 to become the official religion of the Roman state. Opinions differ as to whether this shift represented the triumph of the Church over its persecutors or the victory of political interests over the Church.[1] I am inclined to the latter view, but nothing is simple.

However, the point at issue here concerns the inevitable changes that this shift brought about for Christian thinking.

Having first existed as a minority community, although a growing one, with the state mainly hostile to its existence, the Church had clearly distinguished between itself and the 'world', represented not least by Rome. The opposition of the state had enabled it to maintain its counter-cultural existence with strict expectations concerning non-participation in violence and the dangers of wealth. It was the faith of the powerless. Once established as the religion of the Empire, the 'world' was effectively abolished and declared Christian. The Church then faced questions which it could previously ignore and had to provide a theology for the activities, including violence and hierarchy, by which the state maintained itself. It became the supporter of the powerful. This set up a tension within Christianity which it has never as a whole satisfactorily resolved: would it continue as a religion of radical nonconformity or would it come to terms with the inevitable compromises which managing a fallen world required?

One response to this dilemma is to relate the hard sayings of Jesus on renouncing wealth and violence to the private, interpersonal behaviour of individuals whilst looking elsewhere, perhaps to the Old Testament or to 'natural law', for a philosophy appropriate to public life. The Church then provided a public philosophy but one in which the specifically Christ-centred content was reduced. Questions of discipleship were relegated to a personal, inner realm. The distinction developed that it was the Christian Emperor's duty to take care of the public, temporal realm and the Church's to minister to the 'spiritual' needs of the people. There is, of course, considerable merit in this distinction, provided the two are not made into watertight compartments, since, in fact, there is a continual interaction between personal conviction and public reality. Yet it runs the danger of 'spiritualizing' faith. This split is still evidenced every time politicians of a certain stripe tell church leaders not to 'meddle in politics' but to concentrate on 'saving souls'.

Then came the *Enlightenment shift*. Europe had been torn apart by the wars of religion. The old 'Christendom', in which Church and Empire had continued their alliance for over a thousand years, broke down at the time of the Reformation, both into separate nation states and into territorial churches, each embracing some degree of reform. The potential for international conflict was thus increased and civil wars raged within and between nations as different religious camps strove for dominance. It is understandable that during the Enlightenment religion should be considered a cause of conflict and that the attempt be made to find a foundation for public life beyond the differences of specific religious confessions. Appeal was made to commonly accepted reason. There is much to commend the idea of a 'secular state' where no one is penalized for their religious confession or denied access, for instance to education or public office, because of it. The state which safeguards religious liberty can help to limit conflict arising from sectarian divisions, provided the secular state does not become the 'secularist' state which, while pretending to be neutral, is itself sectarian in that it rejects the value of religion altogether. In this case the strategy of 'privatizing' religion is a way of neutralizing its public influence.

Given a situation where the pressure is on to split faith from public life, some evangelical Christians succumbed, between roughly 1920 and 1960, to a quietist preoccupation with saving souls and effectively withdrew from many areas of social and political concern. This seemed self-evident both in the light of a narrow understanding of salvation and in terms of received political wisdom. Yet it can now be seen to be a form of complicity with the status quo. Not to seek to change the way things are is to agree with them as they stand. The concern for eternal life has sometimes deflected attention and absorbed energies which might well have been directed towards this-worldly transformation. At the same time, it is also important to do justice to earlier evangelical traditions that demonstrated strong social and political concern. The spirit of withdrawal from which evangelicals have been steadily recovering is emphatically not true of many nineteenth-century evangelicals who were at the forefront of social improvement, as many continuing institutions, such as the Shaftesbury Society, Barnardo's, and not least the Salvation Army, still demonstrate.

Analysing sin

Evangelicals have been inclined to see sin as a category of individual responsibility. Social improvement comes about therefore through regenerating and reforming individuals. This is undoubtedly true – in part. Yet developments in the behavioural sciences have caused us to take stock of how individual persons are formed through their relationships with others and of how all of us live out our lives within institutional and social structures which are able to liberate or oppress. The fuller dimensions of human existence need to be seen in the awareness that all social structures are fallen. The remedy for sin must therefore be broader than personal forgiveness. We need to speak the language of 'liberation'.

In fact the wider analysis of sin and fallenness which is stimulated by the behavioural sciences corresponds closely with biblical teaching. The biblical vision of humankind is one in which we are bound together in relationships and community, where the individual person exists in dependence upon others. Furthermore, the New Testament contains clear evidence of the ways in which human social existence is shaped by 'powers and principalities', conceived of as supra-human entities hostile to Christ but overcome by him in his resurrection. The work of Christ is far more than a sacrificial offering for human guilt. It is an act of God whereby he has 'overcome the world' and driven out the 'ruler of this world'.[2] To understand Christ's work adequately all these dimensions need to be taken into account and applied in a holistic doctrine of salvation.

A holistic approach, but . . .

Since World War II evangelical thinking, both in the USA and in this country, has been reconstructing the Christian vision of salvation. The arguments in favour of Christian social and political involvement have overcome resistance to anything which appeared to resemble a 'social gospel'. There is a strong consensus that whereas the need for personal regeneration remains paramount, the gospel must be embodied and expressed in forms of social caring and in the refusal to leave public life to be dominated by anti-Christian philosophies. Mission involves evangelism to proclaim the good news, social action to embody it and political action as both the proclamation of Christian truth in the political sphere and an extension of social action, since the causes and amelioration of social ills are often political in nature. We need to mark these as positive recoveries in evangelical thinking.

Yet those who have argued hard, long and successfully for a new civic responsibility might now have cause for concern, especially at the resurgence of the 'Religious Right' which has emerged as a significant and (to many) threatening force in American politics. Religious conservatives have swung back from their earlier political indifference with a vengeance. It might seem that the spirit of withdrawal has been cast out only to introduce seven worse spirits of religious and political intolerance.[3] Viewed from afar, the Religious Right resembles religious nationalism, convinced about the manifest destiny of the United States under God. Opposition to abortion and euthanasia, and advocacy of capital punishment, and prayer in state schools figure as test issues for America's status as a Christian country: yet they are accompanied by a high commitment to maintaining American readiness for war and by devotion to the 'gun culture' which makes America one of the most violent countries in the world. Once more, Christian moral judgement is skewed towards issues of an individual nature whilst remaining uncritical about wider issues touching upon the corporate fallenness of nation-states.

It is simply my intention here to indicate the ambiguity of the recovery of social and political consciousness among evangelicals. Underlying this is that tension which has never been adequately resolved by the Church since the time of Constantine concerning the very shape of a Christian political theology. To what extent is the Christian faith able to provide an ideology for societies and governments comprised of fallen social and political structures without compromising its own integrity? Is it not the case that the Christian faith will always be in tension with 'the powers that be', never able to 'legitimate' them, but always existing in some sense in opposition to them? And could it ever be right for the Christian Church to seek to advance the purposes of God's Kingdom through control of the powers of state?

Somehow the Church must chart a course between so accommodating to political reality that it loses its own integrity and so maintaining its own distinctiveness that it loses the capacity to address the real world of human compromises. If this were an easy thing to do we should have found the solution long ago. However, certain things ought to be clear.

It should be clear that we cannot put the clock back and reproduce Constantinian Christendom. The development of Christendom was at its best an attempt to assert the relevance of the Christian faith for the public domain and to care with a degree of realism about what happens there. At its worst it allied the Church to the secular power and to the use of violence to compel conformity to the Christian way or to assert ecclesiastical dominance. Its low point was the Crusades, with their inexcusable atrocities perpetrated in the name of Christ. Nothing further from Christ can be imagined. He advanced his cause by surrendering his own life, not by taking the lives of others. In any case, the world has changed and is increasingly pluralist, international and interdependent. The ideal of a 'Christian' nation in the Constantinian sense becomes less and less likely. To the extent that the Religious Right seeks to establish a 'Christian' nation in this sense it will appear to be re-opening the very potential for conflict against which the Enlightenment was a reaction.

Yet nor can we rest satisfied with the Enlightenment option which relegates religion to the private realm. Believing that Christ is Lord of all means seeking to the best of our ability that his will be done in public as in private, and done willingly. If it is true that evangelicals are in political resurgence, and this does seem to be the case in the USA and is claimed for Great Britain although with fewer grounds, it becomes essential to gain proper perspectives on how the political mission is to be pursued. We believe that there has been a missing element in this debate, though one which at least one group of radical evangelicals has attempted to keep alive.

A messianic perspective

That element concerns the marginalizing of the historical figure of Jesus Christ in constructing a political theology. The radical evangelicals who have never lost it are Anabaptist pioneers such as Conrad Grebel, Felix Manz, Georg Blaurock, Michael Sattler and Pilgram Marpeck and their Mennonite descendants. At their best, and like most of us, they often fell beneath it, they made discipleship of Christ a controlling theme for all their thinking.

We noted how the early Church was able to maintain a closeness to the praxis of Jesus because it knew itself threatened by the Roman state. This quite naturally strengthened its sense of conformity to the Lord who was crucified by the Roman authority, a constant reminder of which was the credal clause 'crucified under Pontius Pilate'. The non-violent stance of Jesus was continued and killing in the service of Rome forbidden.

After Constantine, the ethic of a minority group had to be adapted to the majority and to the business of running an

Empire. The theme of the imitation of Christ was then reserved either for personal, rather than political relations, or increasingly for a clerical élite or a monastic discipline. A higher level of imitation of Christ (and this was very much a monastic theme) kept the radical element in the gospel alive while the mass of baptized Christians settled for a lesser level of commitment. This christological focus of monasticism may help to explain its immense influence in the development of Western culture, despite its frequent failings. Increasingly, however, the Church's political theology was shaped by appeal to the Old Testament example of a sacral society, where Church and state are regarded as one, or to natural law, so effectively by-passing Jesus.

We have previously noted how liberal theology stressed the humanity of Jesus and the need to follow his example. Because of the associations with liberalism such language raises suspicions among evangelicals and appears inadequately theological. Yet it is entirely biblical. The New Testament sees the way of Jesus to the cross as determinative for the disciple. We are to have the servant-like mind that was in Christ Jesus,[4] to follow Christ's example of bearing abuse without returning it,[5] to overcome evil with good rather than being overcome by evil.[6] The whole point about the Church is that it is not like the Gentiles who lord it over others, but takes the place of the servant,[7] living by forgiveness not retaliation,[8] loving rather than hating its enemies.[9] Imitation of Christ is directly relevant to the Church which has been called to this task. By derivation, what we learn of God from Christ may be applied to society generally in the hope that it will lead either to its reform, where there is injustice, or to significant alterations to the way in which it fulfils its necessary functions.

Christian political thinking must begin with Christ. In chapter 2 I argued that it is in Christ that God defines himself. God is the Christlike God and Christ's life, death and resurrection define the ways in which he works to redeem the world. Christlike action moves the world forward to its destiny in the new heaven and the new earth. The cross is much more than the way in which redemption is accomplished: it reveals the shape of saving activity. In Christ, God bears and absorbs human hostility and interrupts the vicious cycle of hatred and recrimination which mars human history. He calls Christ's followers to do the same.

It helps here to retrieve a neglected theme in our understanding of Christ, the confession of Christ as Messiah. For Israel this was always a socio-political category. The Messiah would restore the fortunes of Israel and liberate them from the yoke of slavery. Jesus fulfilled the expectation of a political liberator but in a way entirely unique to himself. He came as the one anointed by the Spirit to bring good news for the poor and release to captives. But the means of this liberating work was not the violent overthrow of the Romans, which the Zealots were attempting but which Jesus refused, but the proclamation of the year of the Lord's favour.[10] Hope was not to be found in narrowly political action but in God's coming Kingdom which would liberate and save. Furthermore, the kind of messiahship Jesus exercized was not nationalist and exclusive, aiming at restoring Israel so that she could triumph over her enemies and avenge herself upon them. It was *inclusive* and *merciful*. His intention was that Israel might take up her vocation to serve the purposes of God for all the nations not for herself alone. He incarnated this by both associating with sinners within Israel and showing them God's mercy, and also by reaching beyond Israel to 'unclean' Samaritans and Romans to have compassion upon them.[11]

This focus upon the messiahship of Jesus integrates the personal, social and political dimensions of his mission. He set out to free people to serve God,[12] and this embraced all the ways in which they were held in bondage. The manner in which he did this was distinctive, not employing the forms of political power-seeking available in his social context and involving violence, but gathering his disciples together as a new community living together according to his example of servanthood, forgiveness, non-retaliation and economic sharing. This mission was extended after the resurrection through microsocieties of disciples which interacted with the socio-political order. The prophetic, messianic microsociety of the churches is thus the means whereby God's Kingdom advances and seeks the renewal of the wider society.[13]

The primary political duty

The political duty of the Christian begins with participation in the messianic community of the Church which is the primary instrument God uses to change society. The evangelical insight that the first way to improve society is to work for the conversion of individuals is a partial truth. Conversion is necessary, but it is the transformed community of the Church which is God's basic instrument for changing human communities and which can set an example of how it pleases God when people live together.

The Church is a political community because here we confess one true Lord, and so deny all other totalitarian claims to lordship. Here we are called to live together in love and mutual forgiveness; when we fail, the Spirit of God within the Church keeps the flame burning. How the Church organizes its life becomes a pattern for how human life at large should be lived: taking account of every member, valuing all irrespective of race, gender, culture or class, but not remaining indifferent to sin, seeking not to impose decisions but to gain consent and refusing the right to any other than Christ to be Lord. All communities possess power. The difference in the Church should be that it is conceived first of all as something which is entrusted to individuals, especially leaders, to be used as a form of service to all, not in order to dominate, exploit or gain personal advantage. The Church therefore has political potential in demonstrating a more excellent way to exercise power in the political community. Being the Church is a political act.

Traditionally, evangelicals as an identifiable movement espouse a minimal ecclesiology and tolerate a spectrum of opinions from established Church Anglicans at one extremity to 'sectarian' Anabaptists at the other. Differences over forms of Christian initiation are played down for the sake of evangelical unity. My own conviction is that the Church cannot be considered a second-order issue, precisely because it embodies essential elements of the gospel and the shape of the Church determines what it can offer to society in its holistic mission. Radical evangelicals in the past are apt to have emerged from Free Church traditions such as Baptists, Methodists or Congregationalists. However, all things are in change and there are increasing signs that the values of the radical tradition can be effectively transposed into other traditions in such a way as to maintain those values while still conserving the valuable distinctives of each tradition. Currently this is most evident in some progressive Catholic thinking, especially from within liberation theology,[14] but the trend is also evident in other streams as they come to terms with the demise of 'Christendom'. Radical evangelicals might now be found in the most surprising places.

The line of thought we have been pursuing warns us against hoping for a political salvation. The Constantinian shift was welcomed by some contemporary Christians as the arrival of the millennium. The Emperor assumed quasi-messianic status as the one who would advance the Kingdom of God by means of the power available to him. Remnants of this kind of approach are still to be found in the significance some Christians give to 'Christian civilization', to the belief in Britain or the USA as 'elect nations', or to the reconstituted state of Israel. But when a political entity is accorded messianic status something contrary to the gospel takes place. The Church is an international community which relativizes all states and to surrender to any form of messianic nationalism holds great and divisive dangers. The faithful Church, a supra-national reality, is alone the messianic community.

The Spirit beyond the Church

The Church is the *primary* earthly means of God's liberating work, but not the only one. Just as in the Old Testament God's choice of Israel did not mean that God was inactive beyond Israel,[15] so the Spirit is at work drawing all things through Christ towards their ultimate goal. All the earth is the Lord's and so we trace the Spirit at work beyond the Church, especially in movements that make for human dignity and liberation. To say otherwise would be to believe that there is some other giver of good gifts besides the Lord.[16] Yet history indicates that care must be exercised in the way we discern the 'signs of the time'. In the past, some Christians in Germany and South Africa hailed both Adolf Hitler and apartheid as special providences of God and signs of his governance of history. It takes time to test the true significance of historical events and does the work of God no service when we jump too readily on the latest bus to pass. This is why the Church becomes necessary as an interpreting community, testing in the light of its own witness to Christ the value of new social movements and in the process affirming the good and denying the bad that it sees. But it is not necessary to believe that every good and wholesome impulse needs to have its origin in the Church to be tending in the right direction and worthy of Christian support.

Created, fallen and to be redeemed

The complexities of developing an adequate political theology
either as evangelical or any other kind of Christians come from
the ambiguities of human social systems. They are simultaneously
created, fallen and to be redeemed.[17] Human beings have been
created as social and co-operative beings with the potential to
develop institutions to serve and undergird their corporate life.
This pleases God and is sometimes called the 'cultural mandate',
the human responsibility to create and fashion a cultural envi-
ronment for themselves additional to the natural world. This
capacity is to be respected as creation is to be respected. Yet
human fallenness is such that all social reality extrapolated by
human beings is also fallen and bears the marks of this. If justice
means, following a classical definition, 'to render to everyone that
which is their due', human society fails at the first hurdle by not
corporately rendering to God the wholehearted worship which is
his due. This is what the New Testament means in one of its uses
of the word 'world',[18] the fallen 'system' or world order which
resists God.

Yet the world has been redeemed in Christ and all things will
be reconciled to God through him.[19] The day when 'the kingdom
of this world will become the Kingdom of our God and of his
Christ'[20] is yet future, but is being anticipated in the Spirit's work
in the Church and the world. A great hope for the future therefore gives rise to a modest hope for the present, that the fallen
structures of human social and political existence might no
longer dominate and imprison people but rather serve their
needs and provide a supportive and humanizing context in which
they might seek after God. The Christian task is to recover the
creation God intended from beneath the distortions which our
fallenness has imposed upon it. In doing this, the renewed
humanity and the new social existence which is taking form by the
Spirit of God in the Church, communities of love and service
albeit imperfect ones, can act as a guide in recovering what God
has intended all along for all people. Although not a task which
can be completed until Christ's return to liberate his creation
finally, it can be achieved in part in this age as the Spirit works,
not least through the Church, to humanize the present order of
things. The Church's task includes working towards this end,
being grateful for modest achievements along the way.

A political strategy

We resist the idea that the best way to fulfil the Church's social and political service is to change things by gaining power. Of course, the impetus for creative change must eventually reach the centres of power in order to take lasting effect, but the strategy which begins from the top down is usually flawed. Few truer words have ever been spoken than Lord Acton's dictum that 'power tends to corrupt and absolute power tends to corrupt absolutely'. Not many people can handle power properly. In fact the Church is at its most valuable when it maintains a certain distance between itself and political partisanship and power struggle. Christian faith is concerned with the desirable future, with God's call to the highest and best. Politics is concerned with the art of the possible, with relative judgements and necessary compromises. If the Church *as the Church* pitches itself into this struggle then it can end up giving exaggerated status to limited solutions and discrediting itself. This is the one moment of truth in the Conservative claim that the Church should keep out of politics: in an absolute sense this is impossible since it would mean retiring from life itself, but as a warning about what happens if the Church hitches its star to relative solutions it makes sense. There may indeed be particular issues where a prophetic witness needs to be exercised and a firm stance taken, and there will be a value in the Church's general witness and comment in many areas of legislation, but as a whole the Church recognizes that the political world is the world of limited possibilities, that for all its power, politics is powerless in many things that most matter, especially in creating truly virtuous people.

Yet the fallen world is still God's world and to abandon any part of it is to deny God's claims. The Church evangelizes the people and the culture out of which the political process grows, infusing both with the kind of values which in time will shape political philosophies and politicians. This is a long-term objective. We can, however, distinguish helpfully between the more distant position taken by the Church or churches as such and the political service of individual Christians.

Jesus' description of his disciples as the salt of the earth and the light of the world[21] suggests this distinction. To be the light of the world implies a degree of intensity, the Church as a visible community which embodies the Christlike life. To be scattered as salt suggests the presence of Christians in the world at large, blending in with the surroundings to the point of invisibility. Both these emphases need to be maintained: the Church gathered is distinct from the 'world' and lets its light shine clearly, but, as the Church scattered, individual Christians involve themselves in all legitimate aspects of human society and culture, and work for their improvement. In the dialectic between the Church's standing outside and above partisan politics and individual Christian involvement within the system there is great potential. One allows the possibility of a clear, prophetic witness, the other subverts the false values of the system while giving support to whatever in it might make for goodness and justice.

A useful Old Testament picture here is the contrast between Elijah and Obadiah. To fulfil his prophetic vocation Elijah had to stand over against the ungodly reign of Ahab and Jezebel (and there was no shortage of tame prophets who were willing to tell the king what he wanted to hear).[22] Yet Obadiah, who also 'revered the Lord', was occupying a very precarious position in charge of the king's palace and by doing so was in a position to save a hundred prophets of the Lord from Jezebel's purges.[23] It was right that Elijah as the 'visible' representative of the Lord should be outside the system and equally right that Obadiah as an 'invisible' representative should be within it, both working towards the same end and doing good.

Issues for radical evangelicals

In the light of our discussion, what needs to be said specifically concerning the radical evangelical contribution to the political process?

Only by extending the logic of Christ's mission can we be in continuity with his saving activity. God's action in Jesus Christ is liberating action, in which we see Old Testament themes which take their rise from Israel's exodus experience coming to universal expression. Christ is Israel's and the world's Messiah and potentially brings freedom from all the idols which hold human beings in bondage. God's lordship liberates and humanizes. Evangelicals therefore will be concerned generally both to work for personal conversion, in order that people might be set free from self-bondage, and for liberation from other forms of captivity that are imposed upon people. Freedom from tyranny, unjust structures, exploitation, poverty, abuse, persecution, unfair discrimination will all form part of this agenda.

However, political and social emancipation though desirable are not enough to make a healthy society, both because regeneration is necessary for all and because even when liberation has been accomplished the question remains unanswered as to what kind of people will inhabit such a liberated world. Therefore, although evangelical concern will often correspond to 'enlightened' opinion in general, at this point it diverges considerably. Liberation conceived as an object in itself will prove illusory. In Israel's exodus experience God's liberating actions were directed towards a specific end, namely that Israel might become his own people. Evangelicals will be concerned not only to further human liberation but to see free human beings growing into virtuous citizens who fulfil their obligations to family and community. The Christian vision of freedom is not the freedom to do whatever we please but the will of God, and so to correspond to the destiny for which we have been created. In serving God there is perfect freedom.

Furthermore, radical evangelicals will be realistic about the corrupt and corrupting nature of human power systems. This is where we strike a more radical position. Evangelicals have always had a strong awareness of human depravity. The surprising thing is that this has not always been translated into an equal realism about the power systems of human society. Governments have been deemed capable of good because they are 'God's servants'. Yet fallen and sinful human beings will construct political systems which are at least as sinful as themselves. There is good reason for believing, as was argued in an unsurpassed fashion by Reinhold Niebuhr, that groups of human beings are always less capable of moral good than their individual members.[24] Governments may do some good but not much and not for long. It is for this reason that in democratic systems checks and balances have been created which qualify the unbridled power of the state and require it to serve human beings rather than oppress them. Even in the best of political systems, secrecy and misinformation thrive and vigilance is always necessary.

The radical evangelical tradition has seen this side of the state more clearly because, for instance in the origins of the Anabaptists, legitimate demands for religious liberty were met with state persecution, even in supposedly Christian states.

Dissent from the prescribed state religion was not tolerated. In the cross of Christ it discovered not one single unfortunate mistake but a moment of revelation of what human power systems left to themselves will always tend to do.

Despite this, respect for God's creation necessitates a continuing concern for social and political reality. The idolatry of power does not warrant a rejection of the 'cultural mandate', responsibility for human culture and politics. God has created human beings as social and co-operative beings with the capacity to build institutional frameworks for their existence. These are necessary aspects of human experience and no one lives independently of them. The radical evangelical is concerned to redeem those basic structures of co-operation and mutual service which God has written into his creation. This must begin with existing political options because in the political struggles of the present there are positions which are nearer to or further away from what is believed to be God's will. But the intention of such involvement is to discover those ways in which human beings may best live together.

In this process, the life of the messianic community will disclose insights concerning the world's redemption. If in the Church fallen creatures are discovering healing and entering into a manner of life which more closely reflects God's will for all, that community will at its best fulfil an exemplary function for the wider society. From within the Church the Spirit of God will arise to stimulate creative change in the wider society. Historically this has been the case, with the Church pioneering forms of social caring, healing, education, counselling and social reform. In its radical evangelical form developed first by the Anabaptists then by other Free Churches, the Church has given rise to democratic forms of decision-making, concepts of society as a covenant between free citizens not subjects of an overlord, religious liberty and the concept of the limited state. Consistent with this, radical evangelicals will espouse and further the ideal of societies in which the state plays an enabling not a dominating role, where those who exercise power are held accountable to the people. They will believe, on analogy with the processes of debate and discernment within the congregation, that societies which allow a variety of points of view to check and complement each other are most likely to find acceptable solutions. They will seek to safeguard religious liberty both because the truth of God is able to

bear witness to itself without the aid of government-coerced conformity and because only when the Christian faith is freely
embraced in response to the divine election is it genuine faith.

Radical evangelicals will pursue these ends because such societies most closely resemble the revelation of God in Jesus Christ
and the messianic community he gathered by the Spirit. At the
same time, just as the covenanted community is a disciplined
community which exists under the lordship of Christ and which
establishes through a process of consensus laws and rules for itself
according to what is believed to be Christ's mind, so it will argue
that the civil community which it is seeking to influence rightly
safeguards its stability and security by enacting laws through a
democratic process and enforcing them. Not to do so reduces
liberty to anarchy and so reduces the sum total of freedom. Here
we reach an inevitable limit to the analogy between the local
congregation and the civil community: whereas the Church is
entered by free choice, people have no choice about being born
into society but only that of fulfilling or neglecting their obligations to it; and whereas the Church can rely solely upon the moral
power of persuasion, society possesses the ultimate power to
coerce. Here there is a mutual dependence between Church and
society: faith communities relying upon moral force alone are
able to inspire people to the highest virtues which could never be
won by coercion. They therefore help to form the virtuous and
stable citizens without whom society cannot function. But society,
when it functions properly, possesses the power of coercion by
divine mandate.[25] As the sum total of all its citizens, it is able to
protect its members from criminal and destructive elements and
so to provide the framework within which the work of the Church
and other agencies can take place freely.

Evangelicals: radical or conservative?

There are certain general differences between radical and conservative evangelicals which it would be good in conclusion to
identify.

Conservatives tend to look back to an order of creation which
has been marred by the fall and believe that its remnants must be
preserved. Radicals tend to look forward to the coming Kingdom
of God as proclaimed by Jesus and see it overthrowing the unjust
power structures of the present. One perspective breeds a suspicious

attitude to change and an appreciation of law and order, the other creates an impatience for change and stimulates reform. Conservatives tend to look back to Christendom, the near fusion or close alliance of Church and state, or the idea of a 'Christian country' as the ideal model of Church–state relations. Radicals have doubts about whether the Christendom experiment should ever have been attempted and deny that countries can be Christian in any total sense, although agreeing that there can be greater or lesser degrees of Christian influence. One perspective expects Christian morality to be enforced by legislation upon the population at large. The other sees Christian morality as being first and foremost for the Church and doubts whether a non-Christian population can be coerced into obedience to God's laws.

Conservatives tend to think as though Christians are in the majority and have the right to determine the way things are in society. Radicals know that Christians are in the minority and that the Church's influence will only be as great as its ability to live out its faith. One perspective fears the pluralism of modern societies as a threat to social cohesion and Christian hegemony. The other sees that pluralism as an opportunity to live out and argue its position in a missionary context.

Conservatives tend to see Christian morality in personal and individual terms or as 'family values' and to regard social structures as morally neutral. Radicals are inclined to see social structures as part of humanity's moral crisis and to regard personal morality as one aspect of a wider demand. Both positions agree that Christian faith makes moral demands on the public realm but diverge over questions of what those demands might lead to in social terms and how the Church's moral influence is best exerted.

9

Towards a Generous Religion

There has often been a narrowness and a smallness about the evangelical vision. This book has offered ways in which this might be overcome. Evangelicals would benefit from a paradigm shift enabling them to view the world more hopefully and positively in order to engage with it more effectively. This new paradigm could take up into itself without loss those elements of evangelical witness which represent its faithfulness to Christ and the Scriptures and its realistic appraisal of human sinfulness. This chapter focuses on the evangelical spirit and argues that for Christ's sake evangelical people, churches and institutions should be generous people. Previous chapters have laid some of the theological bases on which such generosity of heart and outlook might be built.

The ambiguity of 'religion'

It is commonplace to deny that true Christianity is in any sense a religion. Following the lead of Karl Barth, many would see God's self-revelation in Christ as God's judgement upon and abolition of 'religion'. Religion is unbelief, indeed the most elaborate of human attempts to hide from God to avoid acknowledging our inability before him, or to seek to reconcile him to us by our own efforts.[1] Fair enough. It is possible, however, to overlook the subtlety of Barth's position which is captured in the German word *Aufhebung*. This word means 'abolition' but also contains the suggestion of 'taking up' something. God's revelation abolishes religion as unbelief but then takes the elements of religion up into itself to establish by grace a true religion which is a divinely enabled response to revelation.

It is illusory to imagine Christianity not to involve forms of religion which can be false or true. The Christian life involves experiences, habits, practices, disciplines and attitudes which are accurately described as religious. They can be humanly generated forms of self-delusion or true reflections of the Christ-filled life. But we cannot be Christians and not embody that commitment in religious forms of one kind or another which the psychologist or sociologist is fully at liberty to investigate under the heading of 'religion'. If evangelicalism is a form of religion it is essential that it become true religion.

At many points in the modern world, religion constitutes a threat to human society, a potential source of division and conflict which sets up absolute loyalties. The news reports bear this out on a regular basis, whether it be a proclamation of religious fatwah against a novelist deemed blasphemous towards Islam; a millenarian sect immolating its members when threatened by the FBI; a doomsday Buddhist cult allegedly releasing deadly poison in the Tokyo underground; a government building being blown up by an apocalyptic survivalist group convinced that the US government are plotting a totalitarian takeover; or Christian or Muslim exorcists being found guilty of gross physical abuse and even manslaughter after applying medieval methods to their victim-clients. All such incidents involve the taking to an extreme of concerns, images or themes which are common to the religious enterprise as a whole. Furthermore, a map of the world's trouble-spots since World War II would reveal how armed conflict frequently occurs where diverse religious traditions encounter each other: Hindu–Muslim, Jewish–Muslim, Christian–Muslim, or even, within religions, competing versions of the same faith. Northern Ireland is the most obvious and immediate instance. Religious loyalties contribute significantly to conflict.

The answer to this perennial problem cannot be to dispense with religion. For one thing, this is an impossibility. The religions of the world may individually wax or wane but they are here to stay for the foreseeable future. The Western perception of the decline of traditional religion is illusory since in global terms Judaism, Islam and Christianity have actually experienced various forms of resurgence throughout this century.[2] Religion will function as a determining social force in shaping the future. Even when traditional religions orientated towards the transcendent are discounted, we are not free of religion. Secular religions or ideologies such as ideological feminism or environmentalism take their place and reproduce the features of the religious mind-set, often at its worst. Atheism is perfectly able to take on religious overtones and to prove every bit as intolerant and persecutory as religion at its worst, as the history of the atheistic regimes of the twentieth century made plain. Secularism can be as dogmatic and sectarian as religion itself. The antidote to false religion is not ultimately no religion but true religion.

Evangelicalism as religion

Evangelicalism cannot avoid being religion. The issue concerns the extent to which it is true religion. Here we are compelled to admit that there is an unlovely side to this often warm-hearted piety. The crux of the matter is how to hold firm convictions with compassion and respect for the dignity of others.

Evangelicalism has the potential to become anti-Christian. As with Luther's belief that the Roman Church of his day was the antichrist, so it could be with evangelicalism. As John indicated, there are many antichrists because antichrist is a 'spirit',[3] an attitude or atmosphere constellated under certain conditions. Religion can find itself in this condition, wittingly or unwittingly opposing the spirit of Christ. The dark side to evangelicalism is prefigured in the religion of the Old Testament and of the Jewish world at the time of Jesus. The grace of God which came to Israel as sheer gift was capable of being construed as a ground for self-righteousness and self-congratulation, as a reason for feeling superior to the Gentile world. Institutions which were themselves the creations and gifts of God such as temple, Torah and sabbath became the basis for a degree of false spirituality and security which would come into conflict with the coming of God in Jesus Christ.[4] The false religion into which Israel had turned the grace of God became liable to judgement as God gave his people over to the consequences of their choices. He sent them into exile as the only way in which they would come to their senses.

The prophecy of Jonah exposes this. Jonah, like Israel, was disobedient to the call of God to proclaim judgement and repentance to the pagan nation. He had excluded in advance the possibility that God should be gracious to those beyond the pale. His period in the belly of the big fish brought him to repentance so that he was restored and given a further opportunity to fulfil the mission. Even so he was reluctant, and when in response to his preaching the pagan people repented, instead of rejoicing he was distraught.

In this prophecy, the compassionate God is in stark contrast to Jonah. The heart of God is wide in its mercy, full of compassion for the lost people of Nineveh and even for their cattle.[5] Here is Jonah's difficulty. He cannot conceive, indeed he dreads and resents the very thought, that God should be so gracious and compassionate.[6] There is a faulty logic at the heart of his religious psyche which believes that for God truly to love Israel he must love less the nations of the world. It is the resolution of this faulty logic which is close to the heart of the distinction between true and false religion. True religion reaches out to others; false religion builds barriers against them. God's love for his elect people is but the first-fruits of his universal compassion. His love for his covenant people is a sign of his love for all creation. God is a burning fire into whose hands it is a terrible thing to fall. But he is also and all the more the God of undying love.

Mapping the dark side

Close to the core of evangelicalism's dark side is the sin of *absolutism*. It is, of course, Christian belief that God is the ultimate reality, that therefore there is final truth and that that truth has taken form in Christ. Yet we must once more clearly distinguish between the absolute which corresponds with God's own being and the human grasp of that absolute reality which is partial until the final revelation of the divine perfection. The nearest points we get to this final reality are in the virtues of faith, hope and love which will eternally remain.[7] There is thus an element of truth in relativism, not that there is no final truth but that human expressions of truth are always capable of being improved. The belief that God has once for all delivered the faith to the saints[8] should not be taken to imply that there is no further room for discussion. The proper challenge is to be faithful to Christian truth claims while being ourselves open to correction.

Absolutism leads to *restrictivism*, the belief that only some are of the truth and beyond their boundaries is little more than error. Some evangelicals draw the circle of the theologically correct as narrowly as possible on the 'tight is right' principle. On an extreme fringe are those who will not eat with unbelievers or professing Christians who are outside their own group. The separatist streak within evangelicalism is pronounced and closely mirrors the tendency of the Israelites to wish to preserve their ritual purity.

'Error' has come to be regarded by some evangelicals as an almost contagious condition with a consequent suspicion both of ecumenical conversations and inter-faith dialogue. The implication is that theological integrity is maintained by keeping at a distance from any group which could be considered heterodox. The result of this is that evangelicals easily live in a bounded world which is maintained by the constant repetition of stereotypes. This must be contrasted with the far healthier if more costly enterprise of face-to-face encounter with those of other viewpoints. Without such contact it is only ever possible to talk past people, to risk misrepresenting their position and to cast them in the role of opponent.

Restrictivism in turn gives rise to *judgementalism*, presuming to pronounce definitively over other people's opinion or status. This is almost an art form among evangelicals who often love nothing more than a good heresy hunt, though it belongs to the form of the art not to admit it. When directed at non-evangelical Christianity it exposes the persistent errors which are to be found there and the impossibility of co-operation without compromise. Until recently, Roman Catholicism was regularly denounced by evangelicals in this way. When directed, as it often is, towards other evangelicals the characteristic motif concerns spiritual and theological 'declension', the departure of the previously sound and healthy from a former orthodoxy. Books are dedicated to this work of exposure, whole denominations are predicated upon it, some preachers thrive on it. Recent examples include biblical inerrancy, opposition to the charismatic movement or movements derived from it, ecumenism, eternal torment, and the role of women. It is a most unlovely form of evangelical faith, not least because those who engage in it believe themselves to be at their most Christian when they are in fact at their most self-righteous. Indeed, they are very often at their least truthful as they fail to do justice to the positions they are opposing or to the persons made in the divine image whom they are called upon to love.

Conviction and compassion

Once more, in the absolutism, restrictivism and judgementalism we have identified we can recognize proper concerns which have become corrupted through lack of humility. Absolutism is a corruption of the Church's nature as a convictional community. Restrictivism is a perversion of the Church's obligation to test all things to discern the truth of God. This is an essential and unavoidable task which is to be applied as much to ourselves as to others. But when the truth becomes a weapon to be used against people, as a means of reinforcing the strangeness of the stranger, we should learn to suspect ourselves. Judgementalism distorts the Church's willingness to have the humble courage of its convictions. It becomes a way in which the boundaries which separate us from others are kept in place by continual reinforcement and a means by which through constantly exposing the shortcomings of others it becomes possible to assert one's own righteousness.

This is the kind of religion Christ came to abolish in order that he might then take up into himself and into our experience of true religion the elements of truth that it contains. The Church is able in the Spirit of Christ and in imitation of him to hold fast to its convictions, to discern the truth and struggle for it in such a way that all of these things may become ministries of compassion for others. There is no contradiction here since the truth sets people free and does them good. It is necessary to explore, however, the ways in which we must avoid false religion for the sake of the true.

The priority of persons

Jesus' saying that the 'Sabbath was made for humankind, and not humankind for the Sabbath'[9] can act as our clue. The practitioners of religion have always the tendency to turn the liberating ordinances of God into ends in themselves which in turn become burdensome obstacles to true religion. People are made subject in importance to religious forms which themselves become all-important. When evangelical faith ceases to be concerned for the well-being of persons and their relational existence it ceases to be a witness to divine love and becomes oppressive religion. Christian faith certainly witnesses to the unique revelation and presence of God in Christ, but that very revelation spells out a love which embraces all and oppresses none. The genuinely Christian style is that which holds firmly to the revelation of God in Christ. But it finds in this not a reason to stand at a distance from others, to erect barriers against them but to draw near and overcome barriers for the sake of God's love for all. This does not mean that the faithful Christian will never find occasion to resist persons or ideas which are destructive. Christ could be as combative as he could be compassionate. But more often than not his fiercest words of condemnation were for the religious who took their religion as an excuse for not having mercy upon others and even this was distinctly his 'strange' rather than his 'proper' work.

Jesus' own approach was to break down the barriers which separated people. His teaching about the free nature of God's forgiveness and his practice of eating and drinking with those very groups regarded as liable to contaminate the 'holy' person are elements of his embodiment of the divine will neglected by evangelicals. It is impossible to hold fast to Christ at these points and maintain the separatist stance which informs some evangelical instincts. Jesus was living out the conviction that people matter to God and love expresses itself by breaking barriers down, not setting them up. This conviction is more concerned for the other than for some supposed religious purity. To live this out, evangelicals would need to become the most generous of people, seeing all, irrespective of race, creed, gender or sexual orientation, as made in God's image and capable of knowing that image restored. The issue is not whether evangelicals believe this, which they certainly do, but whether their religion is true to it.

Evangelicals and religious liberty

My purpose is now to identify certain controlling themes which if generally adopted could encourage the evangelical cause in the direction of generosity. Once more the underlying concern is how to hold together firm conviction with respect for the dignity and personhood of others. We begin with a matter often taken for granted, namely the commitment to religious liberty.

It is characteristic of totalitarian political systems that they assert their dominance by seeking to control through propaganda and ideology the way their subjects think as well as how they behave. Christianity has played this ideological role from time to time, as for instance throughout the years of 'Christendom'. The revelation of God in Christ, in which God's love for all was spelt out, became transposed into a justification of religious compulsion and persecution: Christ was uniquely the way to the Father, all other ways were to be subjugated to this way. This has been the way religion has been employed from time immemorial: the gods of the nations must acknowledge the superiority of the conquerors' god. The propagation of the Christian faith has carried for many, therefore, an overtone which is foreign to its content, that of political domination achieved by force. Christian mission must recognize this and extricate itself from it. This can be done by reconstructing the Christian religion as unambiguously committed to religious liberty.

Within Christianity the radical tradition has from the beginning grasped the incompatibility of compulsion in matters of religious conviction and offered an alternative strategy. There is a certain, forceful logic which proceeds from the conviction of the truth of Christianity to the expectation that as the truth it is the duty of the secular power to believe it and to enforce it. This logic is deeply rooted in evangelicals. Yet it is faulty logic, first of all because Christianity is not primarily a dogmatic system to be imposed but a story to be told, and stories function by inspiration and persuasion not by force; secondly, the imposition of Christian truth contradicts the way in which God in Christ did not impose himself but invited people to the response of faith. Once Christian faith is conceived above all as a truth 'system', the reality of personal relating, which is at the heart of the incarnational principle, is lost.

None of this means that Christianity is entitled to forsake the task of shaping the human social and political order. It does mean that the way in which this necessary 'cultural mandate' is pursued must be through persuasion not by imposition. In a democratic and open society these are, of course, the primary means of influence open to anyone. Even in societies where it becomes possible to gain a Christian consensus about the ways social and political existence are best organized, response in faith to God's grace can only ever be achieved through God's free election and the answering free human response. For this reason it is not only impossible but also blasphemous to attempt to compel people to a response that only God can evoke. The duty of the secular power is to create the framework of stability and order which allows this free interchange to take place.

All Christians insist on the right to believe and propagate their faith. What is not so often grasped is that this very freedom implies the right of others who do not believe or who believe differently to maintain their own freedom. Religious freedom does not work if it is not also freedom for those whom Christians believe to be in error to propagate their error, always provided that the criminal law which protects all of us is respected. I make this point because only when we realize it are we truly committed to religious liberty. To forbid such liberty to others on the grounds that they are in error implies that Christians should be calling the tune about what is decided to be truth and what error. This is where the remnants of the Constantinian mind-set can be found. Yet the liberty of others to pursue their own religious objectives is actually the safeguard of the right of Christians to do the same.

The proposition I have advanced is not an abdication of the responsibility to Christianize society or to seek for the acceptance of Christian truth. The debate concerns *which version* of Christian values we are seeking to assert. I am arguing here for a social order shaped by the values of the radical Christian tradition, the classic 'Free Church' vision which is now shared by many others. From the emergence of the Free Churches in the sixteenth and seventeenth centuries this has been a consistent witness concerning the kind of social order which most closely accords with the way of Christ. Here there is a degree of correspondence with the values of the Enlightenment, at which time the concern for a 'secular' state, religious tolerance and human rights to protect individuals from state domination began to emerge. I believe these to be desirable values. They need to be transposed from their Enlightenment context of the enthronement of reason and of doubt about the possibility of knowing theological truth and relocated in a positive appreciation of the way of Christ. Here they can be grounded and given a foundation not in scepticism but in conviction concerning ultimate reality and its nature as revealed in Jesus.

The implications of this position are that societies should respect the value of religious conviction, that all should be guaranteed freedom of belief and practice, that the right to argue, persuade and evangelize is the test of whether this freedom is real. Evangelicals will rejoice in such freedom and use it to the full. But its corollary is that they should be in the forefront of affirming not the content of positions they believe to be mistaken but the right and freedom of those who disbelieve or believe otherwise to pursue their own way. In this way evangelicals can assert a stance which is unambiguously *for* others and not *against* them. The boundaries to such support are observance of the criminal law and respect for the principle of religious liberty itself. Religions or ideologies which wish to take it away will find themselves steadfastly but lovingly opposed by evangelical Christians.

Conviction and tolerance

Here we need to make a careful distinction which is often obscured. The commitment to religious liberty does not mean that we then become indifferent to matters of religious truth, only that the framework of freedom within which such matters can be passionately debated has been secured. The debate in the public realm concerning which values will shape our life together must then take place. The sincere conviction that others are wrong and that there is a better way is not of itself intolerant. This needs to be said because passionate conviction is sometimes portrayed as religious intolerance and this is not necessarily so. It is nonsensical to claim that we have to agree with others before we can be nice to them.[10] At the same time, conviction about the truth frequently does mean that we lose sight of the person or persons with whom we are debating and seek to override them. The proper Christian blend is one in which firmly believed convictions combine with Christlike respect and concern for our partners in dialogue despite the disagreements that may exist. Martin Buber long ago argued that if God relates to us in an I–Thou rather than an I–It fashion, this style is the most effective in pursuing and arguing the truth with others.[11]

Tolerance is an ambiguous quality since there are many things which ought not to be tolerated and because it is often rooted in indifference. But in so far as it points to a loving way of dealing with others and of listening to them (and love is more clearly a Christian virtue), it is to be nurtured. We go on to make suggestions which are particularly relevant to evangelicals in order that their demeanour may match the content of their message.

Positive suggestions

- We should deal with other people on the ground of a common humanity. If other people are estimated on the basis of whether or not they are Christians we are likely to end up dividing humanity into tribal camps. All people are made of one; they are made in the divine image and exist as persons. We share together a common fallenness and yet exist in a world where the grace of God is made known for all.[12] Christian people are bound in solidarity with others. Goodness is goodness, and truth is truth, wherever we may find them. Although Christians believe in their distinctive vocation, it is one received by grace and not by merit, and even as they are shaped by the Christian communities to which they belong they are also utterly dependent upon the wider community for their well-being.

• We should deal with people on the basis of our common questions rather than our differing answers. Human beings live as questioned creatures and struggle to make sense of their existence. We have been created to feel after God and to find him.[13] It is possible to appreciate that quest as we see it evidenced in others even while not agreeing with the answers others believe themselves to possess. At this level there is room for common feeling between those who are separated by otherwise diverse answers and even with those who offer a non-religious response to their condition. No positions are so irrevocably fixed that a person might not have a change of mind. Furthermore, it is salutary to remember that in apparently rejecting Christianity people are often rejecting what they have been presented with by the Church, and this can frequently be sub-Christian in quality.

• Consequently, Christian convictions should be held firmly but with due modesty and self-criticism. In fact where there is intolerance and undue dogmatism, these can be signs of lack of conviction concealed by a defensive attitude. True conviction is able to allow the truth to vindicate itself. It is necessary to hold firmly to what we believe while continuing to acknowledge that we might be mistaken. This is so not because Christ is questionable but because our grasp of him continues to be fallible.[14] Christ's own manner of approach to us allows room for us both to seek the truth and to doubt it. Christian communication needs to appreciate this factor and style itself accordingly.

• Finally, evangelicals would do well to appreciate the value of living on the boundaries. By this I mean that our own knowledge of God is developed in boundary situations where we know ourselves to be questioned and even threatened. Where this is not the case we live in a comfortable world where our complacencies and illusions are never challenged. The missionary existence of the Church is by definition a boundary existence where continually we are encountering that which is strange and contradictory. We have already referred to the apostle Peter's new insight into the gospel gained through encounter with the household of Cornelius. As a devout Jew the evidences of God's working among the Gentiles surprised and no doubt disturbed him. Yet this became a moment of spiritual and theological progress. So it will continue to be, as evangelical people appreciate that the missionary encounter with people and with cultures is a necessary source for challenging old bigotries and granting new insight into the significance of the gospel which has been given to us and yet which we are far from exhausting.

Conclusions and prospects

There is no doubt that evangelical faith is a force to be reckoned with, that it will outlive and out-thrive many of its critics and that it will help to shape the future of humankind. We have argued that to do this healthily, to be true religion rather than false, it needs to attend to its own theology and attitudes. We have outlined significant points at which this may be done and have called the position we are feeling after that of the 'radical evangelical'. Evangelical conviction has the potential to be a primary source of warmth, compassion and generosity in an impoverished world. It is to be hoped that it will fulfil this mission and destiny to the glory of God and for the healing of the human race.

Notes

1 In Defence of Labels

1 David Bebbington, *Evangelicalism in Modern Britain: A History from the 1730s to the 1980s* (London, Unwin Hyman, 1989), pp. 2–17.

2 Gabriel Fackre, 'Evangelical, Evangelicalism' in A. Richardson and J. Bowden (eds), *A New Dictionary of Christian Theology* (London, SCM Press, 1983), pp. 191–2.

3 Fackre, 'Evangelical', p. 191.

4 See e.g. Jim Wallis, *Agenda for Biblical People* (London, Triangle, 1986), pp. 43–9.

5 Nigel Scotland, *Charismatics in the Next Millennium* (London, Hodder and Stoughton, 1995).

6 Tom Smail, Andrew Walker and Nigel Wright, *Charismatic Renewal: The Search for a Theology* (London, SPCK, 2nd edn, 1995).

7 R. F. Lovelace, *Dynamics of Spiritual Life: An Evangelical Theology of Renewal* (Exeter, Paternoster Press, 1979), pp. 289–336.

8 C. Calver, I. Coffey and P. Meadows, *Who Do Evangelicals Think They Are?* (London, Evangelical Alliance, 1993), p. 11. The twelve tribes are: Anglican Evangelicals, Pentecostals, Ethnic Churches, Renewal Groupings in the denominations, Separated Evangelicals, Reformed Evangelicals, Evangelical Majorities in the denominations, Evangelical Minorities in the denominations, Non-denominational Groupings, the New Churches, the Independents and Evangelical Denominations.

9 D. J. Tidball, *Who Are the Evangelicals? Tracing the Roots of Today's Movements* (London, Marshall Pickering, 1994), pp. 17–18.

10 David Sheppard, *Bias to the Poor* (London, Hodder and Stoughton, 1983).

2 Revolutionary Orthodoxy

1 Heb. 1.3.
2 John 1.18.
3 Luke 10.22.
4 John 20.28; Rev. 5.11–14; 6.9–17.
5 Hos. 11.8.
6 Isa. 63.9.
7 Eph. 2.22.
8 H. Küng, *Christianity: The Religious Situation of Our Time* (London, SCM Press, 1995).
9 Friedrich Schleiermacher, *On Religion: Speeches to its Cultured Despisers* (Cambridge, Cambridge University Press, 1988); *The Christian Faith* (Edinburgh, T. and T. Clark, 1960).
10 See e.g. John Hick, *God has Many Names* (London, Macmillan, 1980); J. Hick and P. F. Knitter (eds), *The Myth of Christian Uniqueness* (London, SCM Press, 1987).
11 Hick, *Many Names*, pp. 51–2.
12 See P. Griffiths and D. Lewis, 'On grading religions, seeking truth, and being nice to people – A reply to Professor Hick', *Religious Studies*, 19 (1993), pp. 75–80; G. D'Costa, *John Hick's Theology of Religions: A Critical Evaluation* (New York and London, University Press of America, 1987).
13 Daphne Hampson, *Theology and Feminism* (Oxford, Blackwell, 1990).
14 Hampson, *Theology and Feminism*, p. 2 and *passim*.
15 Hampson, *Theology and Feminism*, pp. 169–73.
16 A. Freeman, *God In Us: A Case for Christian Humanism* (London, SCM Press, 1993).
17 Freeman, *God In Us*, p. 19.
18 For elaboration, see A. Rasmusson, *The Church as Polis: From Political Theology to Theological Politics as Exemplified by Jürgen Moltmann and Stanley Hauerwas* (Lund, Lund University Press, 1994), pp. 26–9, 39, 42–5.
19 J. H. Yoder, 'On not being ashamed of the gospel: Particularity, Pluralism and Validation', *Faith and Philosophy*, 9/3 (July 1992), pp. 286–7, 289.
20 1 Cor. 1.23.
21 *The Forgotten Trinity 1: Report of the BCC Study Commission on Trinitarian Doctrine Today* (London, British Council of Churches, 1989).
22 John Zizioulas, *Being as Communion: Studies in Personhood and the Church* (London, Darton, Longman and Todd, 1985); 'The Doctrine of God the Trinity Today: Suggestions for an

Ecumenical Study', *The Forgotten Trinity 3: A Selection of Papers Presented to the BCC Study Commission on Trinitarian Doctrine Today* (London, British Council of Churches, 1991), pp. 19–32.

23 *Forgotten Trinity 1*, p. 16.
24 *Forgotten Trinity 1*, pp. 19–25.
25 *Forgotten Trinity 1*, pp. 27–34.
26 *Forgotten Trinity 1*, p. 37.
27 *Forgotten Trinity 1*, p. 41.
28 1 Cor. 1.22–4.
29 C. Gillis, *A Question of Final Belief: John Hick's Pluralistic Theory of Salvation* (Basingstoke, Macmillan, 1989), p. 174.
30 2 Kings 6.16.

3 God's Universal Outreach

1 Heb. 10.27.
2 Luke 16.26.
3 2 Pet. 3.12.
4 1 Thess. 1.10.
5 Zech. 3.2.
6 M. Noll, *The Scandal of the Evangelical Mind* (Grand Rapids and London, Eerdmans and IVP, 1994), p. 22.
7 A. Sell, *The Great Debate: Calvinism, Arminianism and Salvation* (Worthing, H. E. Walter, 1982).
8 Matt. 25.31–46.
9 1 Cor. 4.7.
10 J. Calvin, *Institutes of the Christian Religion*, III.21.5.
11 Calvin, *Institutes*, III.21.6.
12 John 1.29.
13 1 John 2.20.
14 1 Tim. 4.10.
15 Matt. 22.14.
16 Acts 13.46.
17 Luke 13.24.
18 Matt. 7.14.
19 B. Ramm, *After Fundamentalism: The Future of Evangelical Theology* (San Francisco, Harper and Row, 1983), p. 170.
20 C. Hodge, *Systematic Theology: Volume III* (London, James Clarke, 1960), pp. 879–80. Hodge was followed in this by B. B. Warfield, 'Are They Few That Be Saved?', *Biblical and Theological Studies* (Philadelphia, Presbyterian and Reformed, 1952), pp. 334–50.
21 John 1.3–4; Col. 1.16; Heb. 1.1–4.
22 Gen. 1.2; Ps. 104.30.

23 John 1.3.
24 Heb. 1.3.
25 John 1.14.
26 Heb. 9.14.
27 Rom. 1.4.
28 Eph. 1.14.
29 2 Pet. 3.13.
30 Rom. 8.21.
31 K. Barth, *Church Dogmatics: The Doctrine of God*, Volume II/2 (Edinburgh, T. and T. Clark, 1957), pp. 1–506.
32 Mal. 1.2–3.
33 Isa. 42.1, 6.
34 John 3.8.
35 Eph. 1.4.
36 Gen. 6.6; Exod. 32.12, 14; 1 Sam. 15.35; Jer. 18.8, 26.13.
37 J. Orr, *The Progress of Dogma* (London, Hodder and Stoughton, 1901), pp. 292, 294–5.
38 2 Pet. 2.9.
39 Luke 10.22.
40 Eph. 1.4.
41 Acts 3.21.
42 Mark 10.23–7.
43 L. Newbigin, *The Gospel in a Pluralist Society* (London, SPCK, 1986), pp. 88, 175–6.
44 K. Barth, *Church Dogmatics: The Doctrine of Reconciliation*, Volume IV/3:2 (Edinburgh, T. and T. Clark, 1962), p. 810.

4 Scripture: Freedom and Limit

1 See on this Noll, *Evangelical Mind*, pp. 109–45.
2 1 Cor. 14.9–12.
3 2 Tim. 3.16.
4 H. Berkhof, *Christian Faith: An Introduction to the Study of the Faith* (Grand Rapids, Eerdmans, 1979), p. 62.
5 1 Cor. 15.14.
6 Luke 10.30.
7 Heb. 1.1–2.
8 Rom. 5.12.
9 See on this E. B. Davis, 'A Whale of a Tale: Fundamentalist Fish Stories', *Perspectives on Science and Christian Faith*, 43 (Dec. 1991), p. 234.
10 P. R. Ackroyd, *Exile and Restoration* (London, SCM Press, 1968), pp. 244–5.

11 Matt. 12.40.
12 G. M. Marsden, *Reforming Fundamentalism: Fuller Seminary and the New Evangelicalism* (Grand Rapids, Eerdmans, 1988), p. 152.
13 Prov. 1.1.
14 1 Tim. 1.2; 2 Tim. 2.2; 2 Pet. 1.1.
15 See on this the analysis and proposals for reconstruction of W. J. Abraham, *The Divine Inspiration of Scripture* (Oxford, Oxford University Press, 1981).
16 2 Tim. 3.15.
17 This seems to be the tendency of John Stott in D. L. Edwards and J. Stott, *Essentials: A Liberal–Evangelical Dialogue* (London, Hodder and Stoughton, 1988), pp. 103–4.
18 N. T. Wright, 'How can the Bible be authoritative?', *Vox Evangelica*, 22 (1991), pp. 18–23.
19 1 Cor. 1.30.

5 The Creative Redeemer

1 Noll, *Evangelical Mind*, p. 133.
2 A recent and popular demonstration of this is the runaway success among evangelicals of books of fiction such as *This Present Darkness* (Eastbourne, Kingsway, 1989) and *Piercing the Darkness* (Eastbourne, Kingsway, 1990) by Frank Peretti.
3 1 Cor. 1.23; Gal. 5.11.
4 John Stott, *The Cross of Christ* (Leicester, IVP, 1986), pp. 133–63.
5 E. W. Grensted, *A Short History of the Doctrine of the Atonement* (London, Longmans, Green and Co., 1920), pp. 1–10.
6 Mark 10.45.
7 G. Aulen, *Christus Victor: A Historical Study of the Three Main Types of the Idea of the Atonement* (London, SPCK, 1931).
8 Lev. 16.
9 Anselm, 'Why God became a Man' in E. R. Fairweather (ed.), *A Scholastic Miscellany: Anselm to Ockham* (Philadelphia, Westminster Press, 1956), pp. 100–83.
10 Calvin, *Institutes*, 2:12–17; 3:1, 21–4.
11 E. Brunner, *The Mediator* (London, Lutterworth, 1934), p. 152.
12 Isa. 28.21.
13 Isa. 54.8.
14 D. M. Baillie, *God was in Christ: An Essay in Incarnation and Atonement* (London, Faber and Faber, 1948), pp. 190–7.
15 P. S. Fiddes, *Past Event and Present Salvation: The Christian Idea of Atonement* (London, Darton, Longman and Todd, 1989), pp. 109–11, 171–89.

16 E.g. Rom. 2.5; 5.9; 1 Thess. 1.10; Rev. 19.15.
17 C. H. Dodd, *The Epistle of Paul to the Romans* (London, Moffat, 1932).
18 A. T. Hanson, *The Wrath of the Lamb* (London, SPCK, 1957).
19 Fiddes, *Past Event*, pp. 88–96.
20 T. S. Smail, 'Can One Man Die for the People?' in J. Goldingay (ed.), *Atonement Today* (London, SPCK, 1995), p. 88.
21 C. E. Gunton, *The Actuality of Atonement: A Study of Metaphor, Rationality and the Christian Tradition* (Edinburgh, T. and T. Clark, 1988), p. 188.
22 For a creative exploration of these themes see J. Moltmann, *The Crucified God: The Cross of Christ as the Foundation and Criticism of Christian Theology* (London, SCM Press, 1973).
23 V. White, *Atonement and Incarnation: An Essay in Universalism and Particularity* (Cambridge, Cambridge University Press, 1991), p. 53.

6 The Legacy of Liberalism

1 A. Schweitzer, *The Quest for the Historical Jesus: A Critical Study of its Progress from Reimarus to Wrede* (London, A. and C. Black, 1910).
2 H. R. Niebuhr, *The Nature and Destiny of Man: A Christian Interpretation. Volume 1: Human Nature* (London, Nisbet and Co. Ltd, 1941), pp. 190–220.
3 Phil. 2.6.
4 1 Cor. 15.45.
5 Heb. 4.15.
6 Luke 2.52.
7 Heb. 5.8.
8 Rev. 1.5; 3.14.
9 Luke 3.2.

7 A Kinder, Gentler Damnation?

1 Cp. Luke 13.23.
2 H. E. Guillebaud, *The Righteous Judge: A Study of the Biblical Doctrine of Everlasting Punishment* (Taunton, Phoenix Press, 1964); B. F. C. Atkinson, *Life and Immortality* (Privately published, no date).
3 Ex. 21.23–4; Lev. 24.20; Deut. 19.20. These much misused 'eye for eye, tooth for tooth' sayings are not intended to legitimate vengefulness but to establish the idea of proportional and maximum punishments.

4 J. L. Kvanvig, *The Problem of Hell* (Oxford, Oxford University Press, 1993), pp. 130, 135–61.

5 Kvanvig, *Problem of Hell*, pp. 139–48.

6 1 Cor. 15.28.

7 E.g. 2 Cor. 5.8.

8 Matt. 10.28.

9 1 Tim. 6.16.

10 1 Cor. 15.53.

11 Matt. 7.11.

12 E.g. recently D. Pawson, *The Road to Hell* (London, Hodder and Stoughton, 1992); J. Blanchard, *Whatever Happened to Hell?* (Darlington, Evangelical Press, 1993); and the reissued E. W. Fudge, *The Fire that Consumes: The Biblical Case for Conditional Immortality* (Carlisle, Paternoster, 1994).

13 See on this E. Boring, *Revelation* (Louisville, John Knox Press, 1989), pp. 57–9.

14 G. A. F. Knight, *Isaiah 56–66: The New Israel* (Grand Rapids and Edinburgh, Eerdmans and Handsell Press, 1985), pp. 118–19.

15 See also Matt. 5.29–30; 10.28; 18.9; 23.33; Mark 9.47; Luke 12.5; 16.19–31. In the latter parable of the rich man and Lazarus Jesus was adapting a well-known story of reversal after this life to illustrate his preaching of the Kingdom. The primary point is that by hardening our hearts in this life we shape our destiny in the world to come. The degree to which it can be taken in detail as descriptive of life beyond death is dubious, as the reference to lying by Abraham's side (at the feast) should indicate.

16 Rev. 1.8.

17 Isa. 44.6.

18 Isa. 6.5.

19 C. S. Lewis, *The Great Divorce* (London, Geoffrey Bles Ltd, 1946), p. 72.

20 Matt. 8.12.

21 John Hick, *God Has Many Names*, (London, Macmillan, 1980), p. 44.

22 Acts 14.17.

23 2 Pet. 3.19.

24 1 Pet. 2.5.

25 Col. 1.20.

26 Rom. 10.14.

27 This approach is developed in V. White, *Atonement and Incarnation* (Cambridge, Cambridge University Press, 1991).

28 See also the cautionary words under note 15.

29 Heb. 9.27.

30 Rom. 2.5–16.
31 Gen. 18.25.
32 See for a thorough discussion J. Sanders, *No Other Name: Can Only Christians Be Saved?* (London, SPCK, 1994) and C. H. Pinnock, *A Wideness in God's Mercy: The Finality of Jesus Christ in a World of Religions* (Grand Rapids, Zondervan, 1992).
33 Matt. 11.11.
34 Luke 3.16.
35 Ez. 36.24–38; Joel 2.28–32, cp. Acts 2.14–21.
36 Acts 10, esp. vv. 34–5.

8 Radical Politics

1 A. Kee, *Christ versus Constantine: The Triumph of Ideology* (London, SCM Press, 1982).
2 John 12.31; 16.33; see also my *The Fair Face of Evil: Putting the Power of Darkness in its Place* (London, Marshall Pickering, 1988), pp. 155–71.
3 Cp. Matt. 12.43–5.
4 Phil. 2.5.
5 1 Pet. 2.21–4.
6 Rom. 12.21.
7 Matt. 20.24–8.
8 Matt. 5.38–42; 21.21–35.
9 Matt. 5.43–8.
10 Luke 4.18–19.
11 M. J. Borg, *Conflict, Holiness and Politics in the Teaching of Jesus* (New York and Toronto, Edwin Mellen Press, 1984), pp. 195–9.
12 W. R. Shenk (ed.), *The Transfiguration of Mission: Biblical, Theological and Historical Foundations* (Scottdale, Herald Press, 1993), p. 12.
13 L. Miller, 'The Church as Messianic Society: Creation and Instrument of Transfigured Mission' in Shenk (ed.), *Transfiguration of Mission*, pp. 130, 139.
14 Notably L. Boff, *Church, Charism and Power: Liberation Theology and the Institutional Church* (London, SCM Press, 1985); *Ecclesiogenesis: The Base Communities Reinvent the Church* (Glasgow, Collins, 1986), but see also H. Küng, *The Church* (London, Burns and Oates, 1967). Both Boff and Küng have, as is well known, fallen foul of the Vatican.
15 Compare Amos 3.2 and 9.7.
16 Jam. 1.17.

17 W. Wink, *Engaging the Powers: Discernment and Resistance in a World of Domination* (Minneapolis, Fortress Press, 1992), p. 52.
18 E.g. John 14.30; Eph. 6.12; 1 John 2.15.
19 Col. 1.20.
20 Rev. 11.15.
21 Matt. 5.13–16.
22 Compare 1 Kings 21.17–29 and 22.5–6, 13.
23 1 Kings 18.3–4.
24 R. R. Niebuhr, *Moral Man and Immoral Society: A Study in Ethics and Politics* (London, SCM Press, 1963).
25 Rom. 13.1–5.

9 Towards a Generous Religion

1 K. Barth, *Church Dogmatics Volume 1/2: The Doctrine of the Word of God* (Edinburgh, T. and T. Clark, 1956), pp. 297–325.
 2 G. Kepel, *The Revenge of God: The Resurgence of Islam, Christianity and Judaism in the Modern World* (Oxford, Polity Press, 1994).
 3 1 John 2.18; 4.3.
 4 Jer. 7.4; Mark 2.27.
 5 Jon. 4.11; B. W. Anderson, *The Living World of the Old Testament* (London, Longman, 1973), pp. 524–6.
 6 Jon. 4.2.
 7 1 Cor. 13.13.
 8 Jude 3.
 9 Mark 2.27 NRSV.
10 Griffiths and Lewis, 'On grading religions', pp. 75–80.
11 M. Buber, *I and Thou* (Edinburgh, T. and T. Clark, 1937).
12 Matt. 5.45.
13 Acts 17.27.
14 G. Tinder, *The Political Meaning of Christianity: An Interpretation* (Baton Rouge, Louisiana State University Press, 1989), pp. 125–30.

Index